ENCOUNTERING GOD
AT THE ALTAR

ENCOUNTERING GOD
AT THE ALTAR

DANIEL TOMBERLIN

ISBN-13: 978-1533154439

ISBN-10: 1533154430

DanielTomberlin.net

DEDICATION

In memory of my father

MAJOR DOBBY TOMBERLIN
1935-2006

and my brother

RANDALL SCOTT TOMBERLIN
1962-2013

ABBREVIATIONS

BIBLES

ESV	*English Standard Version*
NJB	*New Jerusalem Bible*
NKJV	*New King James Version*
NLT	*New Living Translation*
NRSV	*New Revised Standard Version*

BOOKS

BD	*Book of Doctrines*
BM	*Book of Minutes: A compiled history of the work of the General Assemblies of the Church of God*
GI	*Book of General Instructions for the Ministry and Membership*

PERIODICALS

AF	*The Apostolic Faith*
AP	*Azusa Papers*
CE	*Christian Evangel*
COGE	*Church of God Evangel*
FS	*The Faithful Standard*
LRE	*Latter Rain Evangel*
PE	*Pentecostal Evangel*
PHA	*Pentecostal Holiness Advocate*
WE	*The Weekly Evangel*
WW	*Word and Witness*

CONTENTS

PREFACE

This book is an abridged version of *Pentecostal Sacraments: Encountering God at the Altar* (2015) which was written as a theological introduction to Pentecostal sacramental worship for an academic audience. The book has been well received, and I am grateful.

However, many pastors have suggested that I prepare an edition for the general reader that could be used in the local church as a small group study. With that in mind I have prepared *Encountering God at the Altar*. This book is much shorter in length. I have excluded the academic footnotes, theological language, and references to Greek words. Also, I have removed the supporting writings of the ancient and medieval theologians. The writings of early Pentecostals are essential in understanding Pentecostal spirituality. Therefore, this edition maintains most of the references to their work. When referencing these writers I have used parenthetical documentation and abbreviated the sources. I have rewritten portions of the manuscript for a general audience.

I am hopeful that by providing an edition for the general reader many Pentecostal worshipers will discover a new appreciation for the sacred acts of worship.

Daniel Tomberlin
Pentecost 2016

1

Encountering God at the Altar

Pentecostal altar services are as a tempest with a crash of trees uprooted, rocks loosened and rushing down declivities, frightened birds and beasts fleeing before it and crying out; its confusion and tumult as if God did rend the mountains and come down. It's a combination of tempest, fire and earthquake, then the still small voice of the unknown tongue that witnesses that another has been baptized for duty and called to service, to thanksgiving and to adoration. Glory! Glory! Glory!! (COGE, 1 Jul 1910).

In my spiritual journey, there are sacred places where I encountered God — the Baptist church where I was saved, and the altar where I was baptized in the Spirit. My wife and I met God at an altar and affirmed our marriage vows to each other. A few years later, we dedicated our sons at the altar. Over and over again, I have found myself at an altar to meet with God.

As a child reared in a Pentecostal church, there were many times that we gathered around the altar to "pray through" to salvation, sanctification, and baptism in the Holy Spirit. I have vivid memories of the shouts of joy and cries of lament coming from the praying saints at the altar. On occasion, I would hear someone scream — a scream that would cause my skin to crawl — and I knew that one of the sisters had been touched by God. These altar calls were not just demonstrations of emotionalism, they were sober and life transforming. We didn't really have church unless we had a good altar call.

Throughout the Old Testament, altars were built as a sacred place where God was encountered. The ancients did not think that God's presence was limited to these sacred places. The prophets of Israel affirmed that God is omnipresent. "Holy, Holy, Holy, is the Lord of hosts, *the whole earth is full of His glory*" (Isaiah 6:3). Altars were places where God was encountered. God does not need altars, but humans do. Humans need a sacred place to meet God, because humans are creatures of time and space. For early Pentecostals the altar was the center of divine activity. J.W. Welch declared, ". . . man's way to God leads him to the altar first." He explained,

> The altar was God's way for the people to approach him. It lifted Israel into fellowship with God. Christ is seen in the altar as God's way for us into fellowship with himself. At the altar men come into contact with the character of God. Here, too, they are brought face to face with the claims of God. God is seen to be a Holy God (WE, 8 Apr 1916).

The altar is a place of sacrifice. The people were instructed to bring their offerings and give them to God. The blood of the sacrifices was sprinkled upon the altar and atoned for the sins of the people. The cross upon which Jesus Christ was crucified was an altar. Upon that altar the Son of God was nailed and offered as a sacrifice for the sins of the world. The blood of the Savior was poured out upon the cross and was sprinkled over the face of the earth. Humans are called to come to the cross, to be sprinkled by the blood of Jesus Christ for our salvation and sanctification. As we come to the altar, we are called to present ourselves to God as "a living and holy sacrifice, acceptable to God" (Rom. 12:1). Many Pentecostals spoke of the altar as the place of complete consecration to the service of God. A member of the 1906 Azusa Street revival testified,

> But when I made a complete sacrifice to God— all on the altar— bless God, He really did sanctify my soul, and gave me the real evidence; the witness of the Holy Ghost that the work was done, and the carnal mind was destroyed . . . (AP, 2011).

At the altar we die. The altar is the sacred place where men and women are called "to surrender themselves to be crucified with Christ" (WE, 15 Aug 1916). Worshipers placed themselves "on the altar before God a completely yielded sacrifice" so that "the Holy Ghost can operate on us, renewing spirit, mind, and body" (WE, 23 Sep 1916). To believe in Christ is deny ourselves and take up his cross (Matthew 16:24), "to be dead to sin" (Rom. 6:11), and "to die with Christ to the elementary principles of this world" (Col. 2:20). The altar is a struggle for many because it is a place of sacrifice and death. Many Pentecostals have testified to being "slain in the Spirit" or "falling under the power of God" at the altar. Yahweh told Moses, ". . . no man can see me and live" (Exodus 33:20). To encounter God's glory at the altar signifies the death of the old, fallen person. *The Apostolic Faith*, the official paper of the Azusa St. Mission in Los Angeles, explained:

> It is so blessed to be sanctified, cleansed, *crucified, nailed to the cross of Christ. Old things have passed away, the old man is crucified, slain, and Jesus Christ is enthroned in the heart* and crowned within. He sits upon the throne of our heart, reigning as a king, swaying His scepter of righteousness and true holiness, and keeping the heart clean and pure from sin. Then you are just ready to receive the baptism with the Holy Ghost and fire (AP).

Nellie Gilbert of Benton Harbor, Michigan testified, "I was slain under the power of God. The dear Holy Ghost entered His temple with much shaking of the flesh, but, oh, the peace and joy and glory that filled me since Jesus came to abide" (AP). From Colorado it was reported,

> On Good Friday and Easter Sunday the power of God was especially manifest in Denver, reminding one of the word which says that "in that day the slain of the Lord shall be many" for those convicted fell under the power of the Holy Spirit as people used to do in Wesley's days and were lying on the floor. In this position they seem to commune with the Father, unconscious of their immediate surroundings, some are all broken up and cry to God with intense

3

earnestness, many receiving the blessing they need at His hands and rising full of the joy of His presence and the assurance of their acceptance (AP).

To be "slain in the Spirit" also signifies resurrection and new life in Christ. Worshipers "*arose* with shining faces speaking in the power of the Holy Ghost in unknown tongues" (AP). In Knoxville, Tennessee a "young woman . . . a medium . . . confessed that she was under control of this awful power and wanted to be delivered from it." It was reported that the "demon was cast out in the name of Jesus . . . She fell seemingly lifeless, *then came up shouting the victory, her face shining with the love of Jesus*" (COGE, 11 Apr 1914). At the altar "old things passed away; behold, new things have come" (2 Cor. 5:17).

Our sacred places are sacred because of the presence of God. Our altar may be the family coffee table, or bedside. We can build an altar around a hospital bed as we gather to pray for the sick. The altar is constructed primarily of two things — space and time. If we are to encounter God at a sacred place, then we must set a time and place for that meeting. When God made the covenant with Israel God commanded that an altar be erected (Exodus 20:22-25). The altar was to be a sacred place — a place where God's name was recorded and the people could encounter God and receive a blessing. Many such places are mentioned in the Old Testament. Many of these places have the name of God, *El* or *Yah*, as prefix or suffix to the name of the place. These sacred places give us a space and time where God is encountered.

YAHWEH YIREH

Abraham was on a journey, moving from one place to another. Abraham was a person who responded in faith to the call of God. Everywhere he went, Abraham built altars. Each of these altars defined his spiritual journey. These were the sacred places where God met with Abraham and places where Abraham called on God.

The Lord appeared to Abram and said, "To your descendants I will give this land." So he built an altar there to the Lord who had appeared to him. Then he proceeded from there to the mountain on the east of Bethel, and pitched his tent, with Bethel on the west and Ai on the east; and there he built an altar to the Lord and called upon the name of the Lord (Genesis 12:7-8).

The altar was a memorial where Abraham celebrated his covenant relationship with God. Abraham and his descendants would live in obedience to God, and God would bless Abraham by making him the spiritual father of many nations. In Genesis 12, God made a fivefold promise to Abraham: *I will* show you a land; *I will* make you a great nation; *I will* make your name great; *I will* bless those who bless you; and, *I will* curse those who curse you. Every time Abraham approached an altar, he was reminded of God's promises. The altar became a testimony to the faithfulness of God. Worship at the altar meant that Abraham continued to look for the fulfillment of God's promises.

Most Pentecostals were saved at an altar. The gospel was proclaimed, the Spirit convicted and called, and the sinner responded by *going forward* to the altar. That sacred place where the sinner kneels to confess sin and accept Jesus as Lord is a memorial to God's saving grace. Just as Abraham returned again and again to the altar, so the obedient believer should return to the altar. It is the place where we call upon the Lord, always *going forward* in our spiritual development. The altar call provides the time and space for us to meet with God once again, to call upon God that we might renew our commitment, to be sanctified, or to pray through to the baptism in the Holy Spirit. Pentecostal worship has always been about *movement*. We pray that the Spirit will *move* among us. We come to church expecting to be *moved* by the Spirit. At some point in the service, we are invited to *move* from our seats to pray at the altar.

The altar is the place where Abraham "called on the name of the Lord." A few years ago my wife's family gathered around a hospital bed to be with her one hundred-year-old grandmother as she was dying. When Mama Bill exhaled her last breath, the family began to weep. At the same time, sounds of joy and laughter were heard in the next room. As our family mourned the death of a precious family matriarch, the family in the next room was rejoicing over a new baby. Life and death, as well as joy and sorrow, represent our spiritual journey. One family would make the journey to church to remember and mourn a life lost; the other family would make the journey to church to celebrate a new life. The altar is a place of joy and sorrow.

We will call upon the name of the Lord in our times of joy.

> Oh give thanks to the Lord, call upon His name; make known His deeds among the peoples. Sing to Him, sing praises to Him; speak of all His wonders. Glory in His holy name; let the heart of those who seek the Lord be glad (Psalm 105:1-3).

When a sinner repents at the altar, the angels of heaven rejoice. The saints rejoice when a seeker is baptized in the Holy Spirit, or when someone testifies to being healed. As a young man and woman come to the altar to give themselves to each other in marriage, their families weep with tears of rejoicing. At the altar, we celebrate the passages of life.

Also, we will call upon the name of the Lord in our times of distress.

> I call upon the Lord, who is worthy to be praised, and I am saved from my enemies. The cords of death encompassed me, and the torrents of ungodliness terrified me. The cords of Sheol surrounded me; the snares of death confronted me. In my distress I called upon the Lord, and cried to my God for help; He heard my voice out of His temple, and my cry for help before Him came into His ears (Psalm 18:3-6).

Pentecostal spirituality has suffered the loss of lament in prayer. We have been erroneously told that our victory in Christ means that we will not suffer hardship. If we encounter distress, by faith we should make a positive confession and put a smile on our faces. But that is not the testimony of the Scriptures. In the Scriptures, when faithful people were distressed, they tore their clothes, put ash on their heads, and cried out to God. These prayers of lament were not faithless acts; they were cries of faith. In their distress, they did not turn their faces from God, but toward God. They insisted that God turn His face toward them. This is passionate, meaningful prayer.

The altar was a place where Abraham's faith was sorely tested. "Then they came to the place of which God had told him; and Abraham built the altar there and arranged the wood, and bound his son Isaac and laid him on the altar, on top of the wood" (Genesis 22:9). God had asked Abraham to offer his only son, Isaac, as a sacrifice. The altar always costs something. Remember, at the altar we die. Isaac had been Abraham's greatest joy. The name Isaac means "laughter." Abraham laughed when the angel announced that he and Sarah would have a son. We can only imagine the joy and laughter that Isaac brought to his aged parents. Isaac represented the fullness of Abraham's relationship with God. Isaac was the fulfillment of God's promise. The death of Isaac meant the death of God's promise. Living the life of faith is always a struggle. Faith sometimes requires great risk. It requires that the believer trust in the faithfulness of God, even in the most difficult times. As Abraham approached the altar with a heavy heart, he spoke words of faith: "God will provide for Himself the lamb . . ." (Genesis 22:8).

The altar is the place of God's provision. As Abraham raised the knife over Isaac, he heard the voice of the angel: "Do not stretch out your hand against the lad" (Genesis 22:12). As he looked up, he saw a ram caught in the thicket by its horns. He offered the ram as a sacrifice upon the altar that had been built for Isaac. As the flames of the sacrificial fire consumed the ram and the smoke of the fire danced toward heaven, we can imagine the sounds of joy and laughter as Abraham and Isaac worshiped God. Abraham named the altar "*Yahweh Yireh*," that is, God provides. At *Yahweh*

Yireh, Abraham experienced the depths of despair. He brought to the altar his greatest treasure—his son. In his act of faithfulness, he discovered the faithfulness of God. Abraham's place as the father of faith was firmly established only after he offered Isaac. The angel of the Lord said, ". . . because you have done this thing and have not withheld your son . . . I will greatly bless you" (Genesis 22:16-17). The altar of *Yahweh Yireh* is a memorial to God's commitment to bless the nations of the earth. Here at *Yahweh Yireh*, despair gives way to hope, anguish gives way to laughter.

The Pentecostal altar is place where the sounds of "holy laughter" may be heard. Many Pentecostal worshipers have testified to receiving overwhelming joy and subsequent laughter that could not be restrained.

> . . . while sitting in the meeting on Azusa Street, I felt my throat and tongue begin to move, without any effort on my part. Soon I began to stutter and then out came a distinct language which I could hardly restrain. I talked and *laughed with joy far into the night.* Praise His name for such *a wonderful experience of power and love and joy* (AF, Nov 1906).

> Some were so filled with the Spirit that they acted and talked like drunken men. Some prophesyings that we are not to despise. talking in other tongues, dancing, shouting, running, leaping, crying and *laughing were frequent demonstrations* (COGE, 23 May 1914).

> I am still praising God for victory in my soul and for the Holy Ghost that gives me such blessed peace. Sometimes *He floods my soul with such joy* that it seems like I can hardly stay on this earth. One night at the Antioch church *the saints were rejoicing* and speaking in tongues, and speaking about the coming of Jesus, and *it filled my soul and heart with a holy laughter* and it seemed the time was so near and so real that I could hardly stay in the church. I felt such drawing or His love; I know it is only a foretaste of what it will be when He does come . . . (COGE, 15 Oct 1910).

The joyful demonstrations of dancing, shouting, and holy laughter signified the presence of the Holy Spirit much the same way that tongues-speech was the evidence of baptism in the Spirit. A. J. Tomlinson explained that the diverse Pentecostal manifestations were expressions of the Holy Spirit's joy.

> There are times when the Spirit wants to laugh. He finds a person who is willing to be made a gazing stock and He laughs through that person till He is satisfied. And during the time of it the person is so happy that there is no language to describe it. Inexpressible and full of glory! The Holy Spirit is without a body, so He uses the bodies of men and women for His happiness. This is a mystery, but surely the Holy Ghost is happy when He finds a body to dwell in that will give Him complete control.

Likewise worshipers "dance for joy under the power of the Holy Spirit." The Spirit moved upon worshipers who testified, "My feet got happy." Also, "talking in tongues is a happy experience. The tongues and vocal organs get happy" (FS, Sep 1922). According to Tomlinson, human bodies are the Spirit's means of expression. The Pentecostal encounter was often described using the words of Paul: "The kingdom of God is . . . righteousness and peace and joy in the Holy Spirit" (Rom. 14:17).

"WOE IS ME"

> . . . I saw the Lord sitting on a throne, lofty and exalted, with the train of His robe filling the temple.

> Seraphim stood above Him, each having six wings: with two he covered his face, and with two he covered his feet, and with two he flew. And one called out to another and said, "Holy, Holy, Holy, is the LORD of hosts, the whole earth is full of His glory."

> And the foundations of the thresholds trembled at the voice of him who called out, while the temple was filling with smoke. Then I said, "Woe is me, for I am ruined!

Because I am a man of unclean lips, and I live among a people of unclean lips; for my eyes have seen the King, the LORD of hosts."

Then one of the seraphim flew to me with a burning coal in his hand, which he had taken from the altar with tongs. He touched my mouth with it and said, "Behold, this has touched your lips; and your iniquity is taken away and your sin is forgiven" (Isaiah 6:1-7).

In the year King Uzziah died (742 B.C.) Isaiah entered the holy of holies in the Jerusalem Temple to worship. As he worshiped, he was lifted into the Holy of Holies in the Temple of the New Jerusalem. Isaiah was overwhelmed by the glory and holiness of God. Throughout the Scriptures, a sense of dread, or fear, is common to those who encounter God. Adam and Eve sought to avoid their daily encounter with God because of their sinfulness (Genesis 3:8). The people of Israel feared to hear the voice of the Lord lest they be consumed by the fire of God's glory (Deut. 5:22-27). The apostle Paul wrote that God "dwells in unapproachable light, whom no man has seen or can see" (1 Tim 6:16). When Isaiah described what he saw in the heavenly Holy of Holies he could not explain the essence of God's self. The Psalmist declared that God is covered with a garment of light (Psalm 104:2). The essence of God is brighter and more glorious than even the brightest of the created lights. God's essence is so bright that the light with which God is clothed must be covered by a "thick darkness" (Ex. 20:21; Deut. 4:11; 5:22). Job asked, "Will not His majesty terrify you, and the dread of Him fall on you?" (Job 13:11). Divine presence inspires awe, fear, and dread among the righteous and sinner alike. This is exactly what we encounter as we read the book of Acts. Luke repeatedly tells us that the presence of the Holy Spirit provoked believers and sinners to experience the fear of the Lord (Acts 2:43; 5:5, 11; 9:31). Fear of the divine presence inspires the righteous to self-examination and confession of sinfulness. But the unrepentant sinner seeks only to hide from God (Rev. 6:16).

This brings us to Isaiah's second response to the divine presence — the conviction of sinfulness. He cried out, "Woe is me, for I am ruined! Because I am a man of unclean lips, and I live among a people of unclean lips; for my eyes have seen the King, the Lord of hosts" (Isaiah 6:5). In the presence of divine holiness, the sinfulness of the creature is exposed. We tend to resist this exposure, for we do not wish to see ourselves as we truly are, nor do we wish for others to see us as we truly are. Just as Adam and Eve tried to cover their exposure by leaves, we prefer to cover our sins in garments of self-righteousness. But the leaves could not cover the sinfulness of the first humans, nor can our garments of self-righteousness cover our own sinfulness. Our efforts in covering our sinfulness lead to destruction and death. When the apostle Peter confronted Ananias and Sapphira with their sinfulness, they responded by trying to cover themselves with lies. If they had confessed and made restitution, then certainly they would have been forgiven. But instead, their efforts to cover their sinfulness ended in their deaths (Acts 5:1-11). The exposure of our sinfulness is necessary to salvation. The only way our sins can be covered is by the blood of the Lamb. The Hebrew word for atonement is *kippur*, which literally means "to cover." In the Old Testament, the altar was covered by the blood of the sacrifice. Likewise, in the new covenant the penitent believer is sprinkled with the blood of Jesus Christ (1 Peter 1:2).

Isaiah's confession of sinfulness brought him before the altar. At the altar, he was anointed on the lips with a fiery coal. The fire of the altar serves as a twofold sign: (1) of God's wrath, and (2) of God's saving presence. The fire of the altar burned perpetually (Lev. 6:12-13). Fire is often used as a metaphor of the wrath of God. Isaiah proclaimed, "By the fury of the Lord of hosts the land is burned up, and the people are like fuel for the fire" (Isaiah 9:19). In Ezekiel, God speaks of the "fire of my wrath" (Ezekiel 21:31; 22:21, 31). But the fire also is a symbol of the sanctifying presence of God. Isaiah was sanctified at the altar. His sins were purged, he was set apart as a prophet, and he was sent to a sinful people. Isaiah's anointing with the fiery coal at the altar of God was an expression of God's wrath towards the sinfulness of the nation, but also of God's intent to provide salvation for the nation. This is why Isaiah is sent from the altar. He has been anointed by the fiery coal from the altar so that he may speak words of judgment and salvation to the nation. Isaiah's encounter at the heavenly altar is not unique.

The apostle John was "in the Spirit on the Lord's Day" and was lifted into the holy place (Rev. 1:10; 4:1-2). The apostle Paul testifies to a similar encounter.

> I know a man in Christ who fourteen years ago—whether in the body I do not know, or out of the body I do not know, God knows—such a man was caught up to the third heaven. And I know how such a man—whether in the body or apart from the body I do not know, God knows—was caught up into Paradise and heard inexpressible words, which a man is not permitted to speak (2 Cor. 12:2-4).

It may be that his ecstatic experience is reflected in the letter to the church at Ephesus. In the opening doxology, Paul writes that God has "blessed us with every spiritual blessing in the heavenly places in Christ" (Eph. 1:3). The "spiritual blessing" is the working of the Holy Spirit. Through the Holy Spirit, believers are lifted into the "heavenly places." God has "raised us up with Him, and seated us with Him in the heavenly places in Christ Jesus" (Eph. 2:6). In Christ and the Spirit, believers enjoy the benefits and status of heavenly citizenship even in this present age. Christian life and worship is experienced simultaneously on the Earth and in the heavenly places. Because Christians are "in Christ," believers are present with Him where He is—seated at the right hand of the Father, that is, in the heavenly places.

"FIRE, FIRE, HOLY FIRE!"

During the days of King Omri, many Israelites began to turn away from their ancestral God and turn to the god of the Canaanites, Baal. With the ascension of Ahab to the throne, the apostasy of

Israel became complete. Ahab's wife, Jezebel, was an enthusiastic patron of the Baal cult. Under her direction, the prophets of Yahweh were relentlessly persecuted. The prophets of Baal were welcomed at the royal court. Altars to Baal were constructed throughout the land. Baal was the Canaanite storm god who was chiefly responsible for the rains and fertility. Baal represented the prosperity of the people. The seasonal rains were the essential lifeline for the agrarian culture of the Ancient Near East. The rains of Baal enriched the land and caused the crops and orchards to bear their fruit. Baal was the god of energy and economic prosperity. The religion of Baal became the economic engine that drove life in Israel.

Suddenly, a prophet appeared whose name was "My-God-is-Yahweh." Elijah's very name was a prophetic challenge to the Baal cult, and to the political fortunes of Ahab and Jezebel. To simply speak the name "Elijah" was to speak against Baal. Elijah's first prophetic words were directed at the heart of the Baal cult. "By the life of Yahweh, God of Israel, whom I serve, there will be neither dew nor rain these coming years unless I give the word" (1 Kings 17:1 NJB). With these words, Elijah killed Baal. The great storm god was unable to produce a single drop of dew. The great rivers were reduced to a trickle, and the streams were dry. The land was barren, and there was a great famine. Throughout the land, the people approached the altars of Baal. They offered sacrifices and cried out, but Baal was silent. There was still no rain.

Elijah boldly provoked a confrontation with the prophets of Baal. Two oxen would be offered: one on the altar of Baal, the other on the altar of Yahweh. Elijah then boldly proclaimed, "The god who answers by fire, He is God" (1 Kings 18:24). Certainly the great storm god, Baal, could muster a bolt of lightning for the sake of his reputation. Also at stake were the reputations of Ahab and Jezebel. The prophets of Baal offered an ox upon their altar. They prayed for hours, but the storm god could not answer with even a distant thunder. Baal's prophets danced around their altar, they shouted, and ceremoniously offered their own blood to attract the attention of Baal. All day long they sought to hear, but Baal never answered. By the end of the day, no one was even paying attention. It was obvious that the great storm god was impotent.

Elijah issued an altar call. As the sun began to set, Elijah prepared to offer his sacrifice.

> Elijah said to all the people, "Come near to me." So all the people came near to him. And he repaired the altar of the Lord which had been torn down (1 Kings 18:30).

As the people of Israel watched, Elijah repaired the altar of Yahweh. For the first time in a generation, the descendants of Abraham approached the altar of Yahweh. Before Yahweh could be heard, before the fire would fall, the altar had to be repaired. After the altar was repaired, the sacrifice was prepared. Then Elijah offered a simple prayer:

> "Yahweh, God of Abraham, Isaac and Israel," he said, "let them know today that you are God in Israel, and that I am your servant, that I have done all these things at your command. Answer me, Yahweh, answer me, so that this people may know that you, Yahweh, are God and are winning back their hearts" (1 Kings 18:36-37 NJB).

The purpose of this entire episode is that God wanted Israel back. Yahweh wanted to be heard. Yahweh wanted to be heard by the prophets of Baal, and by Ahab and Jezebel. But the heart of God was for the people of God—the sons and daughters of Abraham. Suddenly, "Yahweh's fire fell!" All day long the assembled multitude waited to see who would prove to be God. Now there was no doubt. With one voice the people cried out, "Yahweh is God . . . Yahweh is God!" (1 Kings 18:39 NJB). The meaning of "Elijah" — My-God-is-Yahweh — had now become the confession of Israel.

Shortly thereafter, "the sky grew dark with cloud and storm, and rain fell in torrents (1 Kings 18:45 NJB). The drought had lasted three years. Baal was proved to be an impotent fraud. Yahweh answered with fire and rain. With the fire, the faith of the nation was restored. With the rain, the life of the land was cleansed and restored. But none of this could have happened until Elijah repaired the altar of *Yahweh Elohim* — Yahweh is God.

Our God is a consuming fire (Hebrews12:29). Pentecostals often speak of God's presence in terms of fire and rain.

> ... God's presence was often manifested by the appearance of fire. *The appearance of fire has not been infrequent since the falling of the latter rain of the Spirit.* Some have been apparently wrapped in fire. In the case of others it has only appeared to rest upon them a moment and then vanish away (COGE, 1 Mar 1910).

Pentecostals believed the outpouring of the Holy Spirit to be the "latter rain," that is, the restoration of apostolic Pentecost upon the last-days church. The earliest Pentecostals often spoke of the "baptism of the Holy Ghost and fire." Pentecostals were often heard to testify of "Fire! Fire! Holy Fire!!!" (PHA, 22 May 1930). Churches experiencing the Pentecostal revival were "catching the Pentecostal fire" (AP). Fiery manifestations were often reported in Pentecostal services. A. J. Tomlinson wrote:

> At one time as I stepped out to make an altar call, as I lifted my hands, a kind of blue mist was seen by a number of truthful witnesses as it settled down on the congregation, and not a few fell, and either crawled or were carried into the altar. A few times while the words were spoken, the Holy Ghost fell on all that heard the Word. Streaks of fire have been seen as they darted just above the heads of the people in the congregation, like zigzag lightning, and yet not so quick but that it was easily seen by scores of people (Tomlinson, *The Last Great Conflict*, 1913).

On some occasions Pentecostal worshipers literally handled fire. Tomlinson reported of "several instances where fire was witnessed indicating the presence of God in our midst . . . fire has been handled by several parties" and "those engaged in it were never burnt, and it was used of God to . . . lead people to the Savior" (COGE, 19 Sep 1914).

Generations later it seems that the Pentecostal Movement is no longer driven by the fire of the Holy Spirit. The initial Pentecostal ethos of "love not the world" has been co-opted by a different, world-friendly, relevant gospel. Some Pentecostals no longer emphasize the gracious encounters of being "saved, sanctified, and baptized in the Holy Spirit." For these Pentecostals, the goal of salvation is to be healthy, wealthy, and successful. Jesus said, "No one can serve two masters; for either he will hate the one and love the other, or he will be devoted to one and despise the other. You cannot serve God and wealth" (Matt. 6:24). During the days of Elijah, the temptation of Israel was to worship at the altar of Baal. The temptation of our day is to worship at the altar of prosperity. During the days of Elijah, God withheld the rains for three years. Before the rains returned, the altar of Yahweh was repaired, the fire fell, and the people confessed, "Yahweh is God." Could it be that God will challenge the false prophets of our day? Could we face an economic collapse so that once again the people of God will forsake the false god and meet at the altar of *Yahweh Elohim*? Could it be that we must hear again the call of the early Pentecostal prophets?

"YOUR SPIRITUAL SERVICE OF WORSHIP"

God has called all believers to present their bodies as living sacrifices. Paul was very familiar with the Old Testament practices of offering animal sacrifices which were burned upon the altar. He wrote, "I urge you, brethren, by the mercies of God, to present your bodies a living and holy sacrifice, acceptable to God, which is your spiritual service of worship" (Rom.12:1). As Paul penned these words, he may have been reflecting upon the Elijah story—of fire falling from heaven. Here, he offers a new perspective on the practice of worship. For Pentecostals, to be baptized in the Holy Spirit is to be totally consumed by the Spirit. Evangelist W. H. Durham testified,

> . . . suddenly the power of God descended upon me, and I went down under it. I have no language to describe what

took place, but it was wonderful. It seemed to me that my body had suddenly become porous, and that a current of electricity was being turned on me from all sides; and for two hours I lay under His mighty power . . . I literally felt transparent, and a wonderful glory had come into my soul . . . His mighty power came over me, until I jerked and quaked under it for about three hours. It was strange and wonderful and yet glorious. He worked my whole body, one section at a time, first my arms, then my limbs, then my body, then my head, then my face, then my chin, and finally . . . after being under the power for three hours, He finished the work on my vocal organs, and spoke through me in unknown tongues . . . I was conscious that a living Person had come into me, and that He possessed even my physical being, in a literal sense, in so much that He could at His will take hold of my vocal organs, and speak any language He chose through me. Then I had such power on me and in me as I never had before . . . I had a depth of love and sweetness in my soul that I had never even dreamed of before, and a holy calm possessed me, and a holy joy and peace, that is deep and sweet beyond anything I ever experienced . . . (AP).

Spiritual service begins with the transformation of human *being*. As living, fiery sacrifices, we present ourselves to God for service and we become a sacramental means of grace, that is, we become men and women through whom the world may encounter God. Worship is not to be limited to formal rites and confessions, or to anointed sermons, dynamic songs, and long prayer lines. Paul has not defined worship as "a spiritual worship service," but as a life given in spiritual service. Paul exhorted, ". . . be transformed by the renewing of your mind" (Rom. 12:2). When Paul speaks of transformation, he uses the same Greek word used in Matthew and Mark regarding the transfiguration of Jesus. He also used this word in writing to the church at Corinth: "But we all, with unveiled face, beholding as in a mirror the glory of the Lord, are being transformed into the same image from glory to glory, just as from the Lord, the Spirit" (2 Cor. 3:18). Humans corrupted by sin are transformed by the power of the Spirit so that they may reflect the glory of God.

The transformation of being is fully expressed in the renewing of the mind. Paul wrote that the human mind has been given over to a "depraved mind." The depraved human mind does not acknowledge God and is governed by unrighteousness, wickedness, greed, and evil (Rom. 1:28-29). However, a mind renewed by the Holy Spirit enables one to "prove what the will of God is, that which is good and acceptable and perfect" (Rom. 12:2). The mind is renewed and the will of God is discovered as the believer commits to the study of the Word of God.

The renewed mind is characterized by sound judgment. The Greek word Paul used here is used by Mark and Luke to describe the deliverance of the demonized man in the country of the Gerasenes. After Jesus had cast out the demons, the man was in his "right mind" (Mark 5:15; Luke 8:35). Paul also used this word to speak of being "sensible" (Titus 2:6). The corrupted mind of humanity follows after the passions of the flesh, which is an expression of self-idolatry (Rom. 1:24-25). However, those who have been renewed and transformed by the Holy Spirit demonstrate sound judgment in that they do not offer their lives in self-serving, idolatrous practices, but as a living sacrifice to God. Sound judgment is reflected in right worship.

The renewed mind is characterized by faith, that is, we have turned from our idolatrous passions and we now acknowledge God and worship Him. This speaks to a relationship, which has been initiated by God, and to which we correctly respond. Paul's emphasis here is not that some are given more faith than others, but that faith is the common grace by which all believers are transformed. Whether one is a Pharisee or fisherman, Centurion or slave, Bishop or deacon, all must come to God by faith.

Our "spiritual service of worship" is offered to God in the worshiping church. All too often we think of the church as a building, or a location. However, Paul has spoken of the church as the body of Christ, that is, a living organism. We have come to God through a common faith in Jesus Christ. It is our common faith in Christ that provides for the unity of the church. But Paul presses the metaphor to speak of the diversity of the church. We are one body in Christ, we share a common faith, but we are individuals who are diverse. The diversity within the body is not a weakness, but it is essential to the very nature of the body. The diversity of the body extends to race, social and cultural background, and gender. Paul has written, "There is neither Jew nor Greek, there is neither slave nor free man, there is neither male nor female; for you are all one in Christ Jesus" (Gal. 3:28). At the altar, human being, as expressed individually and communally, is transformed to reflect the glory of God.

Pentecostalism is a Spirit-*movement*. Pentecostals favor worship in which the Spirit *moves*. For Pentecostals, worship means experiencing the Holy Spirit in the fellowship of the church. While anointed singing and preaching are highly valued, they are not the goals of worship; they are a means to the desired end—an encounter with God at the altar. It is at the altar that souls are "gloriously saved," converts are sanctified, the sick are healed, and seekers are baptized in the Holy Spirit. Whether these altar calls are noisy and dynamic, or somber and tearful, those who witness and participate in this spiritual worship walk away from the altar deeply moved and inwardly transformed. Pentecostal worship is not simply enthusiasm, neither is it entertainment—it is an evangelistic encounter with God's holy presence. Testimonies were routinely published in early Pentecostal periodicals that demonstrated the centrality of the altar. W. J. Seymour wrote,

> The meeting was then transferred to Azusa Street, and since then multitudes have been coming. The meetings begin about ten o'clock in the morning and can hardly stop before ten or twelve at night, and sometimes two or three in the morning, because so many are seeking, and some are slain under the power of God. *People are seeking three times a day at the altar* and row after row of seats have to be emptied and filled with seekers. We cannot tell how

many *people have been saved, and sanctified, and baptized with the Holy Ghost, and healed of all manner of sicknesses.* Many are speaking in new tongues, and some are on their way to the foreign fields, with the gift of the language. We are going on to get more of the power of God (AP).

W. M. Tallent testified,

> When I would go to church the dear Holy Ghost would warn the people, *so they fell into the altar weeping and crying for mercy.* One man was led in from out in the yard while the Holy Ghost was warning the people . . . *When the altar call was made* he tried to come but could not so some of *the workers assisted him to the altar,* and before the service closed the Lord wonderfully saved him (COGE, 1 May 1910).

J. W. Buckalew reported,

> The power of God is falling here, and *the altar is being filled with hungry souls.* Some have prayed through to victory, and have been saved, sanctified, or filled with the Holy Ghost . . . The devil is howling and the saints are shouting (COGE, 15 Sep 1912).

Worship at Pentecostal altars is often ecstatic, that is, the worshiper is lifted into "heavenly places." Pentecostals often refer to this encounter as "the glory of God coming down." One early Pentecostal believer testified, "There is a heavenly atmosphere there. The altar is filled with seekers, people are slain under the power of God, and rising in a life baptized with the Holy Ghost" (AF, Oct 1906). To speak of Spirit "falling" or the glory "coming down" reflects biblical language (Ezek. 11:5; Acts 10:44; 11:15). The experiences of salvation, sanctification, and Spirit baptism are ecstatic because they are "in the Spirit." The presence of the Holy Spirit brings the believer into fellowship with the Holy Trinity. A foretaste of heaven is experienced at the altar. Louisa O'Neal testified,

... after the sermon the preacher asked if there was anyone who wanted to be sanctified. *I went to the altar again*, with my heart so big and heavy I could hardly walk, but I prayed earnestly to God that if this was the right way He would hear my prayers and cries. . . I felt the presence of the Blessed Savior and was accepting his cleansing . . . In a moment I found myself telling the people I was sanctified. Glory to Jesus! I was so full of laughter, I could not laugh enough (COGE, 15 May 1910).

The Spirit "falls down" so that worshipers may be "lifted up" into heavenly places. But there is more going on than Spirit "falling" or the "glory coming down." Because these experiences are ecstatic, the worshiper is lifted up. This is the *movement* of worship. Worship begins at designated times and spaces. As worshipers come together in singing, prayer, giving, sharing the Word, and sacraments, the Spirit is encountered and worshipers enter "into His gates." The presence of the Spirit makes worship transcend the designated time and space so that "worship in Spirit and truth" becomes an otherworldly encounter. W. J. Seymour described the Pentecostal altar as the place where "the great Shekinah of glory is continually burning and filling with heavenly light" (AP). At the altar where the Spirit is present, worshipers enter the heavenly places.

The altar is a sacred place where the sinner kneels to confess sin and accept Jesus as Lord. It is a memorial to God's saving grace. Pentecostal worshipers regularly return to the altar to call upon the Lord, always going forward in spiritual development. Worshipers often referred to the altar as the place where God was encountered. T. L. McClain wrote,

So I went back the next Sunday, after praying all week; and when *the altar call was made it seemed the power of God was too strong for me and I was in the altar before I hardly realized what I was doing.* After this time I did not care who saw me going to or at the altar; so I did not miss going to the altar for a time . . . (COGE, Mar 1, 1910).

Pentecostal worship has always been about *movement*. The altar call provides the time and space to meet with God, to call upon God for strengthened commitment, to be sanctified, or to pray through to the baptism in the Holy Spirit. Pentecostals pray that the Spirit will *move* among the gathered worshipers. Pentecostals come to church expecting to be *moved* by the Spirit. At some point in the service, worshipers are invited to *move* from their seats to pray at the altar. Sister Haynes reported of a fascinating revival:

> And as the glory of the Lord filled the place, some were leaping, dancing, shouting, and speaking with other tongues. As the Holy Ghost played on the organ, a number would be on the floor dancing under the power. *Sinners came to the altar crying to God for mercy.* The last Sunday night of the meeting while Bro. Lemons was preaching, all at once people began to cry and scream, and *arose from their seats all over the congregation, and came rushing to the altar*, until the entire front and part of the aisles were filled with seekers. Oh, such a scene as it was can't be described, people crying to God and the saints rejoicing. (COGE, 1 Jan 1914).

Pentecostals crawled to the altar, rushed to the altar, fell prostrate at the altar, wept and groaned at the altar, laughed and danced at the altar, and were saved, sanctified, healed, and baptized in the Holy Spirit at the altar.

Spiritual worship is expressed in the observance of the sacraments – water baptism, the Lord's Supper, foot-washing, and anointing with oil. Properly celebrated sacraments are "Bible experiences." As a sinner is convicted by the power of the Holy Spirit and responds to the call to salvation, he moves to the altar and presents himself as a living sacrifice. As living sacrifices, new converts present themselves for water baptism. Believers are nourished at the Lord's Supper. From time to time, believers need to be refreshed, so they return to the altar, presenting themselves as living sacrifices to be refreshed as their feet are washed. Each act of spiritual worship requires the presentation of one's "body" as a "living sacrifice."

2

THE SPIRIT OF GRACE

CHRIST AND SPIRIT IN SACRAMENTS

When the day of Pentecost had come, they were all together in one place. And suddenly there came from heaven a noise like a violent rushing wind, and it filled the whole house where they were sitting. And there appeared to them tongues as of fire distributing themselves, and they rested on each one of them. And they were all filled with the Holy Spirit and began to speak with other tongues, as the Spirit was giving them utterance (Acts 2:1-4).

A. J. Tomlinson, first general overseer of the Church of God, presented the tenets of the Pentecostal "full gospel" as "repentance, sanctification, the Holy Ghost, the church, water baptism, the Lord's supper, feet washing, *and everything else.*" Early Pentecostals were adamant that the "whole counsel of God" must be preached if the power of God was to be manifested. Tomlinson insisted:

God honors his word and he wants us to tell it all. If a part of it is left off it is not the full gospel. We may preach tithes and offerings but if we leave off healing it will not be full. May preach everything else besides feet washing it is not full [*sic*]. It is the gospel of the kingdom, which includes the whole of the teachings of Jesus, that must be preached in all the world for a witness (COGE 13 Jul 1918).

Pentecostal spirituality is expressed as encountering Christ and the Spirit in the Church. The "full gospel" is that God sent the "only begotten Son" *and* the Holy Spirit to redeem those in bondage to sin (John 3:16; 14:26; 15:26; 16:7; Romans 5:5; Gal. 4:4-6). The

23

death, resurrection, and ascension of Jesus prepared the way for the redeemed to receive the fullness of the Holy Spirit. The redeemed are born by the Spirit, matured in the Spirit, and glorified through the Spirit (Acts 2:32-33, 38; Rom. 8:2; Eph. 3:19). God the Father offers a saving embrace to fallen humanity through Jesus Christ and the Holy Spirit.

The goal of salvation is to be *in Christ* and *filled with the Spirit*. This is reflected in the common testimony of many early Pentecostals: "Praise God, I'm saved, sanctified, and full of the sweet Holy Ghost!" Pentecostal theology is the reclamation of true Trinitarian theology. The Spirit has found willing voices among Pentecostals. The Spirit of Pentecost is not the gentle breeze of a silent God, but a noisy "violent rushing wind" that inspires a variety of utterances through the people of God (Acts 2:1-4).

> The Holy Ghost comes to glorify Jesus Christ, and reveals His power to save, cleanse and heal. He reveals the power and value of the blood of Christ. He reveals the weakness and need of humanity. Those who are filled with the Holy Ghost feel their need of God more than anyone else does or can. Nothing can take the place of the Holy Ghost in the life of the believer (COGE, 1 May 1910).

Many Pentecostals affirmed a threefold grace of redemption — saved, sanctified, and Spirit-baptized. Some Pentecostals also joyously testified to being a member of the "Church of God of the last days." From their earliest days, Pentecostals have been committed to the study of Scripture. It was in the study of God's Word they found validation for the Holy Spirit's outpouring they were experiencing. For many early Pentecostals, it was this single-minded devotion to Scripture that assured the restoration of the New Testament church. Therefore, the Spirit-renewed church would be *the church of the Bible* (Tomlinson, *The Last Great Conflict*, 1913). As the church *of the Bible*, the Spirit-renewed church should reflect the life, doctrine, and polity of the apostolic church. Pentecostals justified their faith and practice by the Bible. Speaking in tongues was the initial evidence of the baptism in the

Holy Spirit because it was "the Bible evidence." Converts were to receive water baptism; believers were to partake of the Lord's Supper and wash the saints' feet; church members were to practice tithing; the sick were to be prayed for and receive divine healing— all because "it's in the Bible." Sam C. Perry declared:

> As true followers of the Lord Jesus Christ, we desire in all things to conform to the teaching set forth in the Holy Scriptures . . . The Word of God, our guide, the Christian's only standard, sets forth the doctrines to be held, the experiences to be possessed, the life to be lived, and the service to be rendered to God and our fellow man (COGE, 15 Sep 1912).

As the church *of the Bible*, the church should be devoted to the study of the Scriptures. Pentecostals trusted that the Holy Spirit would give illumination and guide the sincere student of the Word. For Pentecostals, searching the Scriptures is an encounter with the Holy Spirit. One early Pentecostal proclaimed, "This Bible becomes a new book to those baptized with the Holy Ghost" (AF, Jan 1907). Theology is a life lived in obedience to God. Pentecostal theology is not simply a study of God's past revelation; it is also reflection upon God's ongoing revelation.

Pentecostals are committed to the authority of the Bible as the Word of God. The Bible is the authoritative written revelation of God. The Spirit guides the study and proclamation of the Bible. The proper place of this interaction between Spirit and Word is the church. The church is a community of interpreters and no single bishop, teacher, or theologian is an authority unto oneself. The preaching and teaching of one is subject to the discernment of the community of the faithful (1 Cor. 14:29, 32; 1 Thes. 5:19-22; 2 Peter 1:20-21; 1 John 4:1). Pentecostals are very careful to maintain the authority of the Spirit and the Word over the church as the interpretive community.

Through the activity of the Holy Spirit the church is the government of Christ in this present age. The government of the church is *executive* and *judicial*. The church is to rightly *judge* the Scriptures and faithfully *execute* the mission of Christ. The church is the visible and literal presence of God's government on the earth. The rule of the church, through the power of the Spirit, in this present age anticipates the rule of the righteous in Christ's millennial kingdom. The terms "church" and "government" were often synonymous. J. L. Thornhill wrote, "The church is the necessary indispensable pillar and ground of the truth;" and, that membership in "the Bible church" was part of the "divine order" in the Pentecostal way of salvation (COGE, 28 Apr 1923). The church of the New Testament was to reflect proper order, unity of fellowship and mission, a common confession, and the power of the Spirit.

The church is a Spirit-anointed communion and its mission is to proclaim the message of the coming kingdom of God. Spirit baptism is the event by which the church is defined. Tomlinson wrote:

> There are none so hungry for the demonstration of God's great power as those who are nearest to it. From many quarters comes the cry, from Spirit-filled souls, for the manifestations of God's power as was shown in the time of the Apostles . . . The gifts are for the church and they will make their appearance in their fullness and glory as soon as she is freed from the power and dictations of man (Tomlinson, *The Last Great Conflict*).

God has given the spiritual gifts to guide the church in its worship and mission. The mission of the church is to preach the gospel throughout the world, so that the coming kingdom of God can be hastened. The spiritual gifts are given to the church so that lordship of Christ may be exercised in this present age. The gifts of leadership and administration guide the church. The teaching and preaching gifts inform and transform the church. Gifts of miracles and healings demonstrate that the power of the coming Kingdom is within the church in this present age. The gift of exorcism demonstrates that the powers that seek to govern this age are limited and ultimately defeated. The gift of prophecy provokes sinners to repent and acknowledge the lordship of Jesus Christ. The gifts of tongues and interpretation of tongues serve as a sign of the universal nature of God's kingdom. The gift of martyrdom reminds us that we do not fear the powers of this world, but trust in Him who is the resurrection and the life. The gifts of mercy, giving, and voluntary poverty demonstrate the economics of God's kingdom in which the treasures of this age are of value only when governed by principles of compassion and generosity. Empowered by the Holy Spirit, the church is God's "government in exile," awaiting the coming of the King in power and glory.

Proper discernment is the guardian of spiritual renewal. A mature Pentecostal spirituality understands that one's encounter with the Spirit is informed by the Word in a Spirit-filled church. Ray Hughes has offered wise counsel:

> While we are living in the Age of the Spirit, we must not forget that we are also living in the Age of the Church. In times of great spiritual outpourings there is a danger in emphasizing experience to the exclusion of basic truths . . . It is harmful to go beyond the teachings of the Scripture . . . *It is at this point that the Church serves as a guardian of our experience* . . . (COGE, 12 May 1975).

Pentecostal spirituality recognizes the value of discerning elders and bishops who guide the church carefully through seasons of revival, as well as seasons of spiritual drought. The Holy Spirit continuously works in the church so that the church may be renewed throughout the generations. The Holy Spirit preserves the faith of the church, and the Spirit renews the faith of the church. Renewal movements within the church are to be anticipated as the continuing ministry of the Holy Spirit. But all renewal movements must be discerned as being faithful to the teachings of the Holy Scriptures. The desire for renewal should never comprise discernment in the church.

A PROPHETIC COMMUNITY

The church is a prophetic community in which the saving acts of God are revealed to all humanity. God has spoken through the Son and continues to speak through the Holy Spirit. The prophetic nature of the church can be experienced during worship. The apostle Paul wrote, "But if all prophesy, and an unbeliever or an ungifted man enters, *he is convicted by all, he is called to account by all; the secrets of his heart are disclosed; and so he will fall on his face and worship God, declaring that God is certainly among you*" (1 Cor. 14:24-25). As worshipers sing, hear the preached word, and celebrate the sacraments, the Holy Spirit is present, actively searching the hearts of those gathered together. Unbelievers may be profoundly affected by the prophetic Spirit. The Spirit can be grieved or quenched, but one cannot escape the Spirit's searching. The Spirit opens the sinful heart to judgment and the sinner encounters divine grace. Overwhelmed by the Spirit of grace, the repentant sinner worships God in humility and testifies to the saving power of God. The church is a redemptive community through which fallen humanity may receive the transforming grace and power of God.

Due to human rebellion at Babel, human society is broken, confused, and oppressed (Genesis 11:1-9). Humans struggle among themselves creating greater and exceedingly painful divisions. However, John envisioned a redeemed community "which no one could count, from every nation and all tribes and peoples and tongues, standing before the throne and before the Lamb" worshiping God (Rev. 7:9). This community is foreseen in the Jerusalem Pentecost event where the judgment of Babel is corrected. The confused languages of Babel are transformed by the Holy Spirit into ecstatic languages of worship. Pentecost fulfills the reconciling mission of Christ and anticipates the glorification of redeemed humanity. Pentecostal worship is prophetic because it anticipates a redeemed human community where violence and oppression cease. Pentecostals envision a community where "there will no longer be any death; there will no longer be any mourning, or crying, or pain" (Rev. 21:4).

The church exists in this present age as a sojourning community seeking the kingdom of God (Heb. 11:8-10, 13-16). The church is a *waiting* community. Often this waiting is expressed in the lament "How long, O Lord?" How long will the righteous suffer at the hands of the wicked? How long must we live in this corrupt age? How long will God be patient with injustice? This lament expresses the church's certain hope that God will act to install His righteous reign. The church's journey is a tearful pilgrimage of faith and hope. The hope of the church is the hope of the world as well. Paul wrote, "For the anxious longing of the creation waits eagerly for the revealing of the sons of God" (Rom. 8:19). The waiting of the church and creation is expressed as the groans and labor of birth pangs. As the church sojourns in this present age, Spirit leads the way. The church has the "firstfruits of the Spirit' (Rom. 8:23). The word "firstfruits" signifies the Spirit's ministry in sealing and guaranteeing the redemptive work of God. Also, it implies a greater harvest in the future. As the church makes her pilgrimage in this world, she sows the seeds of grace. The presence of the Spirit in and with the church signifies that the church is the hope of the world. In other words, what the Spirit has begun in the church, the Spirit will complete in creation.

THE SPIRIT OF GRACE

The church is a Trinitarian fellowship — Father, Son, and Holy Spirit in fellowship with redeemed humanity. The church is the "body of Christ" filled, empowered, and indwelt by the Holy Spirit. The church is the special dwelling place of God's Spirit on earth. The church is a Trinitarian fellowship in which the Spirit is encountered and grace is received. The Holy Spirit is the "Spirit of grace" (Zech. 12:10; Heb. 10:29). Grace is more than God's affection toward humanity, and it is more than the efficacy of redemption. Divine grace in its fullest sense is the *activity* of God. To be a recipient of God's grace is to encounter the Spirit. Through the *activity* of the Holy Spirit the eternal Word became incarnate in the womb of the Virgin Mary. The union of God the Son with humanity means that, in Christ, human nature exists in intra-Trinitarian fellowship. Likewise, the Spirit of grace makes it possible for humans to be "in Christ" and reconciled to God. In Christ and through the Spirit, redeemed humanity lives in fellowship with the Holy Trinity. Divine grace is the presence and power of God. As the Spirit moves God's people are touched, and filled with grace and power. To be Spirit-filled is to encounter God in "great power" and "abundant grace" (Acts 4:33).

The Spirit endows the church with various spiritual gifts. The spiritual gifts flow from the grace of the Spirit. The gifts of grace are freely given by the Spirit so that believers may "grow in the grace and knowledge of our Lord and Savior, Jesus Christ" (2 Peter 3:18). The spiritual gifts signify the Spirit in action. It was because of "great grace" that the apostles were empowered to witness to the resurrection of Jesus through miracles (Acts 4:33). Because Stephen was "full of grace and power" he performed "great wonders and signs among the people" (Acts 6:8). Again, the grace of God is the activity of the Holy Spirit among the faithful.

The worshipful acts of thanksgiving and blessing are an expression of grace. Jesus and Paul referred to the prayer of blessing, or thanksgiving, at the celebration of the Lord's Supper (Acts 13:50-52; 1 Thes. 1:6; 1 Peter 1:6; 4:13). Paul associates this with "praying in the Spirit" (1 Cor. 14:16-17). The Spirit graces the church with spiritual gifts. The church worships and prays in the Spirit. The life and worship of the church expresses the grace and joy of the Spirit. Samaria became a city of "great joy" because of the works of the Spirit in the ministry of Philip (Acts 8:6-8). Even in the face of great persecution, Spirit-filled disciples of Christ experienced the joy of the Holy Spirit. While imprisoned, the apostle Paul wrote to the church at Philippi: "Rejoice in the Lord always; again I will say, rejoice!" (Philip. 4:4). In this present age, believers are graced with the heavenly fruit of the Spirit — love, joy, and peace (Gal. 5:22). Worship is a joyful and ecstatic experience because as believers worship the Spirit of grace is encountered.

AN EMBODIED SPIRITUALITY

Pentecostalism is an embodied spirituality. Spirit baptism means that human being—flesh and blood, soul and spirit—is immersed in, or interpenetrated by, the Holy Spirit. Further, Spirit baptism means that the Holy Spirit dwells within human being. Believers are filled with the Spirit, and the Spirit is enfleshed in human being. Just as Jesus Christ is "God with us," the Holy Spirit is "God in us."

Early Pentecostals testified to this divine encounter:

> The Holy Spirit descended in clouds of glory, wave after wave of glory broke upon me. Tidal waves of resurrection life and glory surged through every organ of my body, so that I was constrained to cry aloud for everything within me shouted "Glory" and could not be silenced (AF, Oct 1907).

> We had an all-day service . . . In the baptismal service, twelve followed the Lord in water baptism. In the afternoon we had the Lord's Supper and feet washing *with the usual results — shouting and other demonstrations of the Spirit"* (COGE, 7 Jul 1917).

Salvation, understood in terms of being "saved, sanctified, and baptized in the Holy Ghost," transforms human nature and anticipates glorification. Believers are *in* Christ and *shall be like* Christ (1 John 3:2). Spirit baptism means that the Holy Spirit and matter (human body) are joined and that by this joining (infilling) human being is transformed. Redeemed humans are partakers of the divine nature. Pentecostal preachers often encourage their listeners to live holy lives because "your bodies are a temple of the Holy Ghost!" The Spirit-baptized believer is empowered to be a witness to the full gospel of Jesus Christ in this present age.

Baptism in the Holy Spirit is a sacramental encounter, that is, Spirit acting upon physical matter. It is often assumed that Pentecostal spirituality is anti-sacramental. It is true that early

Pentecostals were anti-liturgical, favoring spontaneous worship over the formal worship of traditional churches. However, it is a mistake to assume that Pentecostalism is anti-sacramental. The embodied spirituality of Pentecostalism, expressed in the doctrine of the baptism in the Holy Spirit, suggests that Pentecostalism is essentially sacramental. Pentecostal worship is experiential in a variety of ways. Worshipers sing, shout, clap, and dance. They speak in tongues as the Spirit "gives the utterance" and hear tongues-speech. In prayer, a worshiper may be anointed with oil and prayed for with the "laying on of hands." Pentecostal worship is ecstatic and somatic: that is, "out of the body" or S/spiritual, and "of the body."

One of the earliest Pentecostal statements of faith may be found in *The Apostolic Faith*. This statement of faith includes an exposition on the "three ordinances in the church, foot-washing, the Lord's Supper and water baptism." Foot-washing is "a type of regeneration," and an "expression of humility toward each other in real love." The Lord's Supper has a threefold meaning: (1) the sprinkled blood signifies redemption; (2) "the body of the Lamb eaten for health and healing;" and (3) the Christian Passover, that is, the blood of Jesus Christ "gives us victory over all the powers of the enemy." Water baptism is an essential ordinance because it is commanded by the Lord. Water baptism identifies the believer with the death, burial, and resurrection of Jesus. Believers are exhorted not to reject "the command of our Lord and Savior, Jesus Christ, or these different ordinances that He has instituted." Early Pentecostals embraced these sacred acts of devotion due to their desire to be faithful and obedient to the Bible. They insisted that they were "seeking to displace dead forms and creeds . . . with living, practical Christianity." Their understanding of "living, practical Christianity" included sacramental worship (AF, Sept 1908).

The sacramental essence of Pentecostal spirituality is demonstrated in the worship of early Pentecostal churches. The sacramental practices of praying for the sick by anointing with oil and laying on hands, water baptism, the Lord's Supper, and the washing of the saints' feet were common occurrences. The sacraments were commonly observed in conjunction with Pentecostal revival meetings. At the conclusion of Pentecostal revivals, converts were invited to join the church and receive water baptism; and, the Lord's Supper and foot-washing were observed. Occasionally, healings were reported in conjunction with sacramental worship. W. A. Looney reported from Rising Fawn, Georgia:

> About 33 were saved and nearly all . . . were sanctified and 12 or 15 received the Holy Ghost. I led seventeen down into the water and baptized them while the singing, shouting and talking in tongues were in full force on the creek bank. A large crowd stood and witnessed newborn babies being buried with Christ in baptism. An invalid woman was carried down to the water and baptized. She raised one of her hands and praising the Lord that she had not used for years. Sunday we observed the Lord's Supper and feet washing and one of the sisters reported that the power struck her and she splashed the water nearly out of the pan with her feet and she had not been able to use them for several years before (COGE, 2 Oct 1920).

A REAL PRESENCE

For early Pentecostals, baptism in the Holy Spirit brought into their lives a "real presence" they had not experienced in the churches of the Reformation. Spirit baptism made Jesus a present and living person in the lives of believers. Alex A. Boddy, a British Pentecostal, declared:

> . . . so this same Holy Spirit is the power and the only power, in which we may live out Christ's life on earth, and ever gain the victory over His enemy and ours. He makes the indwelling Christ very real to us (WE, 1 Sep 1917).

Likewise, Sam Perry proclaimed:

> The religion of our Lord Jesus Christ is not merely a life of forms and ceremonies and outward ordinances, but a spiritual force within the human soul. It is true that the outward ordinances, duties, etc., must be attended to, but there is no amount of outward service and show that can be of any profit if the inner heart is not touched with Jesus the source of all life and power (COGE, 2 Feb 1913).

Spirit baptism is the dynamic that transformed the Reformed and/or Wesleyan theology of early Pentecostals into a distinctive Pentecostal theology. Spirit baptism moved theological confession into the realm of spiritual encounter. Spirit baptism transformed Christian worship into a living and dynamic Trinitarian fellowship. This "real presence" extended to the way Pentecostals experienced the sacraments. R. E. Stockton wrote:

> Well, some people are afraid of forms and ceremonies because the Catholics practice them in place of salvation. No! The trouble with the Catholics is they lack the Spirit which makes the ceremonies real, while our Church with the Holy Ghost to back up all we say or do gets blessed and edified greatly in the practice of ordinances (FS, Nov 1922).

Pentecostal sacraments are "essential ordinance(s) of righteousness" (BD). They are to be observed "literally and *in the Spirit* and for the purposes set forth in the Scriptures" (WW, Jun 1915). Early Pentecostals intuitively knew that there is a "real presence" in the celebration of the sacraments. This can be seen in the terminology they used. They would often use the words "ordinance" and "sacrament" in the same writings, as if these words were synonymous. In the early published writings of the Church of God, the Lord's Supper was known as "the Sacrament." Also, even as they explained the Lord's Supper as a memorial, or water baptism in terms of an act of obedience, they wrote (and preached) with a deep sacramental devotion. They intuitively *knew* there was something more.

Observance of the sacraments is among the oldest features of Christianity. Water baptism and "the breaking of bread" are essential to the message and celebration of the church throughout the Acts of the Apostles. Water baptism cannot be separated from the call to repentance (Acts 2:38, 41; 8:12, 16, 36-38; 9:18; 10:47; 16:15, 33; 18:8; 19:3-5; 22:16). The "breaking of bread" cannot be separated from the worshiping community (Acts 2:42, 46; 20:7). The practice of the "laying on of hands" or "anointing with oil" for prayer and healing began with Jesus and is continued in the ministry of his disciples (Mark 6:13; 16:18; James 5:14). Whether or not we understand the mystery of how we encounter the grace of God through the sacraments, we cannot diminish their significance in the life of the early Christian community. To early Christians, participation in the holy sacraments was theology in action.

The Christian faith is expressed in the sacred acts of Christian worship. As believers assemble together to celebrate the Lord's Supper, the church witnesses about the redemptive ministry of Jesus Christ to the unbelieving world. When new converts present themselves for water baptism, they publicly confess Jesus as Lord and testify to new life in Christ. When the elders of the church pray for the sick, the power of the resurrected Lord is demonstrated. Unbelievers who witness the sacred acts of Christian worship see and hear the gospel. Jesus told us that the first commandment is "you shall love the Lord your God with all your heart, and with all your soul, and with all your mind, and with all your strength" (Mark 12:20). Worship is the deepest expression of love for God. Worship as an expression of love must engage all human senses, as well as the mind. Sacramental worship offers the opportunity for the worshiper to see, hear, taste, smell, feel, and reflect. As the church worships in Word and sacrament, believers are nourished and the gospel is proclaimed to the world.

MYSTERY, SACRAMENT, OR ORDINANCE?

So that we may have a clear understanding of the issue before us, we must define the terms *mysteries, sacrament,* and *ordinance.*

The Orthodox theological tradition prefers the word *mystery* over sacrament. This affirms a sanctifying presence of Christ and Spirit in the liturgical rites that defies theological explanation. The substance – bread, wine, water – of the sacraments is "filled with the power of God" which interpenetrates the sacramental substances (Staniloe, *The Sanctifying Mysteries*). The Orthodox concept of mystery transcends the rite itself. Reception of the mysteries unites the worshippers with the Divine life.

The term *sacrament* is defined as "the signs and instruments by which the Holy Spirit spreads the grace of Christ the head throughout the Church which is his body" (*Catechism of the Catholic Church*, 1997). In other words, to receive the sacrament is to receive saving grace. In Roman Catholic theology, the sacraments are the effective agents of God's grace because they are the "sacramental presence" of Christ. As long as the sacrament is received by a priest in apostolic succession, and grace is not resisted, the sacrament conveys redemptive grace.

Many Protestants have rejected the term *sacrament* in favor of *ordinance*. An ordinance is an act of worship ordained by Christ as a visible sign of redemptive grace. Most Protestants limit the number of ordinances to two: water baptism and the Lord's Supper. The term *ordinance* has been preferred over *sacrament* so as not to assign saving grace. God's grace is not received through the ordinance, but directly from God through the act of obedience of the believer. In other words, water baptism does not *cause* the new birth, but is a symbol of redemption already appropriated due to the faith of the believer. The bread and cup of the Lord's Supper merely *represent* the body and blood of the Lord; they do not *become* the Lord's body and blood, and there is no "real presence." When the believer is baptized or partakes of the Lord's Supper, it is merely a symbolic act. Ordinances are observed as obedience to the Scriptures. This view of the sacred acts of worship tends to make them incidental, or even unnecessary. If the sacred acts of worship are not a means of grace, then they are observed rarely, or not at all. It may be that this minimalist view of the sacraments has robbed many Evangelical and Pentecostal churches of a vital source of spiritual life.

Early Pentecostals often used the terms "ordinance" and "sacrament" as synonyms. Even so, some Pentecostals have historically favored the term "ordinance" over "sacrament." A *sacrament* is a sacred act of worship blessed by Christ the High Priest through which the worshiper encounters the Spirit of grace. Sacraments are the priestly gifts of Christ to His church. Sacraments are sacred dramas in which all the faithful are actors in redemptive history. Sacraments nurture and edify believers. Sacraments are significant acts of devotion and discipleship through which believers are sanctified. Proper sacramental worship requires the presence of Christ and the Spirit with the community of believers and a material means—water, bread, the fruit of the vine, oil—through which grace may be received. Understanding sacraments as "means of grace" where worshipers encounter the Holy Spirit should be an easy "leap of faith" for Pentecostals. Pentecostals have believed in the "transfer of divine energy" or a "tangible anointing." Following the example of Scripture, many "anointed handkerchiefs" and other objects have been used to effect healing and otherwise assist in working miracles through the power of the Holy Spirit (Acts 19:11-12). Therefore, if healing can be effected by the Holy Spirit through the means of an anointed handkerchief, could not the consecrated "bread and wine" of Holy Communion convey saving grace when received in faith by the worshiper? Pentecostals describe this as the "Shekinah" of God.

> O that men and women would tarry for the baptism with the Holy Ghost and fire upon their souls, that the glory may be seen upon them just as it was upon the disciples on the day of Pentecost in the fiery emblem of tongues. The tongues of fire represented the great Shekinah glory. So today the Shekinah glory rests day and night upon those who are baptized with the Holy Ghost, while He abides in their souls (AF, May 1908).

The divine glory interpenetrates material realities which are accessible to sanctified humans by the activity of the Holy Spirit. The Holy Spirit *moves* and *rests* upon physical objects such as the bread and cup of Holy Communion, the waters of baptism, or an anointed handkerchief. A Pentecostal sacramental theology implies that the Spirit *moves* upon and interpenetrates the sacramental elements which become a "means of grace" in the context of the worshiping church as Trinitarian fellowship.

CHARISMATIC RITES

Pentecostals have long affirmed that God can effect miraculous healing through the sacramental acts of "anointing with oil" and the "laying on of hands." Because Pentecostals affirm the power of God and the authority of the Holy Scriptures, miracles such as Christ's turning water into wine and the multiplication of loaves and fishes are believed without criticism. It is simply a matter of faith. Is it not also a matter of faith that through the words of Christ and the power of the Holy Spirit, the elements of holy sacraments can be permeated by God's divine energies? Therefore, due to the animating presence of the Spirit, baptismal waters are sanctified, and all who enter by faith are cleansed. In like manner, the Holy Spirit effects the consecration of the "bread and wine" so that by partaking of this simple meal, believers partake of the body and blood of the Savior. Oskar Skarsaune wrote, "The charismatic understanding of the ministries of the ordained clergy therefore corresponds to the dominant role accorded to the Spirit in the Lord's Supper as well as in baptism. Without the Spirit, sacraments would are empty rites, conferring nothing on those partaking. Where there is no Spirit, there cannot be any real sacraments" (*In the Shadow of the Temple: Jewish Influences on Early Christianity*, 2002). Sacraments are charismatic – Spirit-anointed – by nature. Sacraments are spiritual graces and those who participate in faith encounter the "real presence" of Christ through the Holy Spirit. As we approach the altar to participate in sacramental worship, we do so "in the Spirit." The Holy Spirit makes us aware of heavenly realities, and we experience heavenly mysteries.

The relationship between spirit and matter is assumed in the Judeo-Christian worldview. According to the Old Testament, all matter has its source in S/spirit. God is spirit (John 4:24). God, who is spirit, created all matter — the heavens and earth. The Spirit of God moves over creation and is poured out upon all flesh (Genesis 1:2; Joel 2:28). All matter is held together through the power of God (Col. 1:17). In creation, there is an essential and causal relationship between S/spirit and matter. In the womb of the Virgin, Spirit and flesh became permanently united in the person of Jesus Christ. This is important to the way the Spirit interacts with the various sacramental elements. The Holy Spirit rests upon creation and material objects. God is present and at home in creation. God makes all things possible. The waters of the baptismal pool, the bread and cup of the Lord's Supper, and the anointing oil can indeed be sacraments, that is, they are a means through which believers encounter the Spirit of grace. The elements of the sacraments are material substances which the Spirit *touches*. In the observance of the sacraments, believers *touch* the elements and are *touched* by the Spirit. The elements of the sacraments are mediating gifts of grace because of the presence of the Spirit of grace.

The physical aspect of Pentecostal spirituality is evident throughout the Jerusalem Pentecost event (Acts 2). The Holy Spirit descended "from heaven" into this present age, into this physical world. Believers *heard* "a noise like a violent rushing wind;" they *saw* "tongues as of fire." The Divine wind/Spirit "*filled* the whole house;" tongues of fire *rested* upon the believers and they were "*filled* with the Holy Spirit." Believers "began to *speak* with other tongues" and the crowd *heard* "them *speak* . . . in our own language." Peter explained the advent of the Holy Spirit as the gift of Father and Son "which you both *see* and *hear*." Luke tells us that "those who had received his word were *baptized*" and that believers devoted themselves to "the apostles' teaching and to fellowship, to the breaking of bread (*taste, nourishment*) and to prayer." The pathos of the Pentecost event was "*feeling* a sense of awe." Pentecostal spirituality is not simply *spiritual*; it is *encountering* the Holy Spirit with our human senses as the Spirit moves and interacts in our *physical world*. Pentecostalism is a *physical spirituality*. The Pentecostal doctrine of baptism in the Holy Spirit with the initial physical evidence of speaking in other tongues provides the model for understanding Pentecostal sacraments.

SACRAMENTS AND THE *WAY OF SALVATION*

The Pentecostal *way of salvation* is best expressed as a series of subsequent encounters of God's grace. Salvation is a process of spiritual growth within the community of faith. The *way of salvation* begins with the effectual call of the Holy Spirit to draw a sinner to repentance, regeneration, and union with Christ. The *way of salvation* continues in sanctification and Spirit baptism, and is completed in glorification. The Spirit's effectual call comes through the preached Word. The human response is faith demonstrated by repentance and continuing devotion to God. This occurs in the worshiping church.

The church is essential to God's redemptive plan. Many Pentecostals affirm that the *way of salvation* occurs within the church, but the relationship between salvation and church is often neglected. However, if the church is indeed the "body of Christ" and "the fellowship of the Holy Spirit," then Pentecostals must affirm a place for formal initiation into the visible church and participation in the sacraments within the *way of salvation*. Many early Pentecostal evangelists understood this. At the end of their revival meetings, they often extended an opportunity for the newly converted to join the church. In the language of the Acts of the Apostles, revival reports often ended with a report of how many souls were "added to the church" (Acts 2:41).

The church is the "body of Christ" which is filled, empowered, and indwelt by the Holy Spirit. As such, the church is an extension and perpetuation of the Incarnation. Therefore, as Jesus Christ is the incarnation of the eternal Son, so the church is the incarnation of the eternal Spirit. As the incarnation of the Holy Spirit, the church is the "temple of the Holy Spirit" (1 Cor. 3:16; 6:19). The temple of the Holy Spirit is constructed with Jesus Christ as the cornerstone. Spirit-filled apostles and prophets are the foundation stones (Eph. 2:20). Each redeemed human is an "earthen vessel" which contains heavenly treasure — the glory and Spirit of God (2 Cor. 4:7). These human vessels, filled with Spirit are the stones with which the temple of the Holy Spirit is erected. Further, each human vessel is presented as "a living and holy sacrifice, acceptable to God" in the "spiritual service of worship" (Rom. 12:1). As a living sacrifice, each Spirit-filled believer burns with the fire of the Holy Spirit. As a living, fiery sacrifice, believers present themselves to God for service, and this is the highest form of worship. Just as the temple in Jerusalem was the special dwelling place of Yahweh (2 Chr. 7:2, 16), so too, the church as the temple of the Holy Spirit is the special dwelling place of God on the earth.

The church is the spiritual mother of all believers. Just as an infant receives vital nourishment from the breast of its mother, believers receive spiritual nourishment and nurture for proper Christian formation from the church. Although Pentecostals have emphasized various discipleship models (such as Sunday school) from their earliest days, it is the worship service that has been the primary method in which Pentecostals are taught the truths and practices of the faith. The church in worship has a profound impact on believers. The combined effect of anointed biblical preaching, dramatic personal testimonies, and spiritual singing wields a powerful influence on the spiritual nurture of believers.

Participation in the sacramental life of the church is essential in the *way of salvation*. Believers who have the opportunity should joyfully participate in the life and sacramental worship of the church. To disregard the sacraments is gross error, even sinful

(Mark 16:16; John 6:53; 13:8, 14; Jas. 4:17). Some early Pentecostals suggested that failure to receive water baptism after conversion could lead to apostasy. W. G. Anderson offered a compelling defense of sacramental practices in the Church of God, suggesting that those who oppose sacraments are false prophets.

> When we hear men willfully ignoring the holy commandments of the Lord and declaring that holy baptism was only intended for Jews, that observing the holy sacrament is not required for the children of God in these days, that washing the saints' feet is only practiced by the weak-minded and fanatics; and thus fleecing the Immaculate Lamb of every visible ordinance that He has left for his true children to remember His example, to follow in His steps and remember His suffering in having his body broken and his blood shed, we are brought face to face with the Scripture — Many false prophets shall arise . . . Not only are these false teachers cutting out all the sacred ordinances of the Lord Jesus, but they are denying the existence of a literal, visible Church of God in the world (COGE, 20 Apr 1918).

Anderson presented a straightforward Pentecostal belief of church and sacraments. A visible church with visible sacraments is not contrary to Pentecostal spirituality, but essential to it. Christian worship without the preached Word and sacraments cannot be worship in Spirit and truth.

God the Father gave the Son and sent the Spirit as *primary saving gifts*. Through the Son and the Spirit, humans are redeemed and the church is established. In this *way of salvation*, the church and the sacraments are *secondary saving gifts* which proceed from the Son and the Spirit. The sacramental worship of the church is a means of grace through which sinners experience the blessings of salvation. The saving efficacy of the church and sacraments is wholly dependent upon the saving acts of the Holy Trinity.

The call of the Holy Spirit is a call to life together. The Holy Spirit calls us to eternal life in fellowship with the Holy Trinity—Father,

Son, and Spirit. The Spirit calls us that we may share eternal life in the fellowship of the redeemed. Jesus gave us a basic definition of the church: "For where two or three have gathered together in My name, I am there in their midst" (Matt. 18:20). Jesus and Paul insist that the church properly exists as a plural body where individuals are members of one another (Rom. 12:5; Eph. 4:25). When the church gathers to worship, God is present. The celebration of sacraments requires the gathering of believers as a faith community. When a convert is baptized, it is normally in the presence of the worshiping community. When believers gather together around the Lord's Table, it is a community fellowship meal. When a believer takes up the towel and basin, it is done so that another's feet may be washed. Believers who are suffering call for the elders of the church to pray. The observance of sacraments cannot be properly experienced alone, apart from the worshiping community. It is through participation in the worshiping community that the worshiper encounters the Spirit of grace. As the worshiper continues the journey along the *way of salvation* the worshiper grows in the grace and knowledge of the Lord Jesus Christ.

RENEWAL MOVEMENTS

JOHN WESLEY AND THE METHODIST MOVEMENT

John Wesley is considered the grandfather of modern Pentecostalism because of his doctrine of sanctification. Wesley viewed salvation as an ongoing process, stages of growth, which would eventually lead to perfection. Inherent in this sanctifying process were the "means of grace." Wesley understood the "means of grace" to be "outward signs, words, or actions, ordained of God, and appointed for this end, to be the ordinary channels whereby (God) may convey to men, preventing, justifying, or sanctifying grace." The means of grace in Wesleyan spirituality are prayer, study of the Scriptures, and "receiving the Lord's Supper, eating bread and drinking wine in remembrance of Him." The methodical practice of these spiritual disciplines is ordained of God "as the ordinary channels of conveying His grace to the souls of men." The observance of the spiritual disciplines is not seeking salvation by works, because the observances of the spiritual disciplines are acts of faith. Wesley was not concerned with proper liturgical form because "external worship is lost labor" unless the worshiper has "a heart devoted to God." He considered faithless forms of worship to be "an utter abomination to the Lord." For Wesley, there is a distinction between liturgical *form* and true sacramental *worship*. He wrote, "Every believer in Christ is deeply convinced that there is no merit but in Him; that there is no merit in any of his own works; not in uttering the prayer, or searching the Scripture, or hearing the word of God, or eating of that bread and drinking of that cup." The spiritual disciplines are sacramental acts of devotion wholly dependent upon the presence of the Spirit of God and the faithful response of the believer. The goal of these sacramental acts is "a heart renewed after the image of God." Wesley insisted the believer has a "duty of constant Communion." The frequency of Communion "will not lessen the true religious reverence, but rather confirm and increase it."

> The grace of God given herein confirms to us the pardon of our sins, by enabling us to leave them. As our bodies are strengthened by bread and wine, so are our souls by these tokens of the body and blood of Christ. This is the food of our souls: This gives strength to perform our duty, and leads us to perfection. If, therefore, we have any regard for the plain command of Christ, if we desire the pardon of our sins, if we wish for the strength to believe, to love and obey God, then we should neglect no opportunity of receiving the Lord's Supper.

Wesley believed that Christ is spiritually present in Holy Communion. The Holy Spirit administers Christ's atonement to the faithful. Likewise, the Holy Spirit makes Christ present in the Lord's Supper.

> The cup of blessing which we bless, is it not the communion, or *communication,* of the blood of Christ? The

bread which we break, is it not the communion of the body of Christ? (1 Cor. 10:16). Is not the eating of that bread, and the drinking of that cup, the outward, visible means, whereby God conveys into our souls all that spiritual grace, that righteousness, and peace, and joy in the Holy Ghost, which were purchased by the body of Christ once broken and the blood of Christ once shed for us? Let all, therefore, who truly desire the grace of God; eat of that bread, and drink of that cup.

The Wesleyan renewal was a renewal of sacramental worship that affected Christian devotion on two continents for generations. The decline of sacramental devotion within the Methodist Movement may be one of the causes of the loss of vitality in Methodist spirituality.

THE CANE RIDGE COMMUNION

The Cane Ridge Communion of 1801 was one of the greatest renewal movements in the history of Christianity in North America. The Cane Ridge Communion has been called "America's Pentecost" (Conkin, *Cane Ridge: America's Pentecost,* 1990). Following the tradition of the Scotch-Irish Presbyterian immigrants, "the Communion" was a regular event in which many congregations came together for several days. The climax of the event was the observance of Holy Communion. Hundreds, even thousands, usually attended the Communion. The event included preaching, singing, a day of fasting, the Communion day, and concluded with a day of thanksgiving. The regular Communion was often the stimulus for revival and renewal among attending congregations. The Cane Ridge Communion was scheduled for August. There had been many local revivals preceding the Cane Ridge Communion, and there was much anticipation that the Cane Ridge event would be special. Indeed, it was a spectacular event. Most estimates place the attendance at more than ten thousand people. Remember, this is Kentucky in 1801. People traveled to the event on foot, horseback, and in wagons. Necessities, like food and water were of short supply. There were no toilet facilities for humans or animals. Most of the attendees camped in tents, or under the open sky. Several prominent ministers preached simultaneously throughout the day in various locations. It was a noisy, even chaotic event that sounded like a roar for miles around. The Cane Ridge Communion is most notably remembered for the spiritual "exercises" that were manifested. A prominent minister who attended the event, James Campbell, described the spiritual pathos of the Communion:

> Sinners dropping down on every hand, shrieking, groaning, crying for mercy, convoluted; professors [of religion] praying, agonizing, fainting, falling down in distress, for sinners, or in raptures of joy! Some singing, some shouting, clapping their hands, hugging and even kissing, laughing; others talking to the distressed, to one another, or to opposers of the work, and all this at once—no spectacle can excite a stronger sensation. And with what is doing, the darkness of the night, the solemnity of the place, and of the occasion, and conscious guilt, all conspire to make terror thrill through every power of the soul, and rouse it to awful attention [sic].

Not everyone who attended the Cane Ridge Communion actually participated in the Sunday Communion service. Only those who had carefully prepared in the prescribed spiritual disciplines and had Communion tokens could be admitted into the Communion service. The Communion services were orderly events but deeply affected the communicants. Even those who were not given to the more dramatic emotional exercises of the event openly wept at the Communion table. Pentecostals may be surprised to learn that the camp meeting tradition associated with the nineteenth century revivals was actually a later development that began with the regular Communion event. Sadly, the Cane Ridge Communion was the last major sacramental event associated with the camp meeting movement. Even as the camp meeting movement developed, church membership and sacramental devotion declined in American Evangelical churches. Spectacular events have overshadowed local church commitment and sacramental devotion of American Christians. This continues to be a problem, especially among Pentecostal and Charismatic churches.

The Wesleyan and Presbyterian sacramental piety was instrumental in the spiritual formation of those who participated. Congregations, as well as the individual believers within them, were strengthened. These sacramental events were significant for two reasons. First, spiritual preparation included attention to the Scriptures, prayer, and fasting. These spiritual disciplines prepared one's heart, mind, and body for sacramental worship. Second, the participants held to a high view of the sacraments. Christ was really present. They expected a divine encounter. Pentecostals often look back to these renewal movements as proto-Pentecostal.

THE PENTECOSTAL ALTAR

The anticipation of a divine encounter is central to Pentecostal worship. As we have previously noted, many early Pentecostal churches celebrated the sacraments as the climax of a revival meeting. Those who had been converted during the revival were baptized in water. Also, it was customary that the Lord's Supper and/or foot-washing would be observed at the end of the revival. Revival reports published in various Pentecostal periodicals can attest to this practice. Pastor I. H. Marks reported from Ft. Myers, Florida:

> Sunday afternoon four followed Jesus in water baptism and were added to the church. Sunday evening we partook of the Lord's Supper and washed the saints' feet, the Lord met with us, Glory to God! Such leaping, dancing, shouting, and talking in tongues [sic]. We will surely not forget that time soon (COGE, 30 Oct 1915).

Sister Beatrice Roberson reported from Surrency, Georgia:

> The meeting at the Church of God, four miles south of Surrency, Georgia, began July 24 and closed August 12. Three were saved, sanctified and filled with the Holy Ghost, five added to the Church and two followed the Lord in

water baptism. The services were conducted by Brother J.A. Hipps. Brother Earl Paulk was with us a few nights and preached three soul stirring sermons. It was wonderful how the Lord blessed in giving out the Word. Hot lamp chimneys were handled under the power. The Lord's Supper and feet washing was observed . . ." (COGE, 25 Aug 1923).

G. W. Stanley reported from Dry Fork, Virginia:

There were several saved and ten . . . got sanctified . . . about seven got the Holy Ghost, for which I praise God. There were twenty added to the church. We had a baptizing, and there were twenty-one baptized . . . We administered the Lord's Supper and washed feet, and while they were at the altar three got sanctified. While we were taking the bread and wine folks were going through to victory. On that same day there were some making threats and that night they were found in the altar crying to God for mercy. I thank God that among the number my oldest boy and girl got saved and sanctified. My little girl was on her knees at the altar sacrament, just as she drank the wine the Lord sanctified her (PHA, 1 Aug 1918).

The full gospel was preached under the inspiration of the Holy Spirit. Sinners were saved, sanctified, and Spirit-baptized. New converts received water baptism and were added to the church. Believers were blessed as they partook of the Lord's Supper and washed the saints' feet. The Spirit's presence was manifested in dancing, shouting, and tongues-speech. These are expressions of an embodied Pentecostal spirituality which is charismatic and sacramental. As Pentecostal pastors seek to lead their congregations, it might be that a focus on sacramental devotion will prove to be a meaningful and powerful way to Christian formation and spiritual renewal.

The center and focus of Pentecostal worship is the altar. Pentecostal worship is defined by redemptive experiences. In Pentecostal altars, men and women are saved, sanctified, healed, and baptized in the Spirit. Pentecostals attend church to encounter the Holy Spirit. Pentecostal worship without sacraments and the Word may lead to shallow emotionalism. The church must promote worship that affirms the Word and Sacrament in the Spirit. Therefore, the challenge for Pentecostals is to develop and lead worship with a focus on the altar that is a holistic event. In Pentecostal worship, believers encounter the Spirit of grace by participating in God's redemptive events as expressed in the observance of the sacraments. Pentecostal worshipers are informed and formed through Spirit-inspired preaching of the Word. This is how Pentecostals are spiritually formed and discipled. Pentecostal worship is transformative because worshipers encounter the Holy Spirit and are sanctified and Spirit-baptized.

The church, devoted to Jesus Christ and living in fellowship with the Holy Spirit, is a means of grace to all who encounter God in worship. Those who enter the worshiping church encounter the Spirit of grace. God has endowed the church with ministry gifts, empowered by the Holy Spirit, for the purpose of proclamation and spiritual formation (Eph. 4:11-13). As worshiping churches pray in the Spirit and sing spiritual songs, the redemptive power of the kingdom of God breaks forth. This is where sinners are convicted and repent, the sick are healed, and the demonized are delivered as the Spirit imparts "great power" and "abundant grace" to the church (Acts 4:33; 6:8). Through the power of the Spirit of grace, the church is a life-giving community through which saving grace is both dispensed and received. Pentecostal spirituality is expressed in terms of encountering God through Christ *and* the Spirit *in* the church. Jesus Christ is proclaimed as Savior of all and High Priest and Bishop of the church. The church is the body of Christ and the fellowship of the Holy Spirit.

The celebration of the sacraments is an ongoing altar call. For most Pentecostal churches, the altar call is the central event of the worship service. Sinners are encouraged to come forward to the altar to "pray through" to salvation. Believers are encouraged to come to the altar to pray for sanctification, or to "pray through" to the baptism in the Holy Spirit. During the altar service, those who are sick, or otherwise in need, are encouraged to come to the altar. There the church elders will anoint with oil, lay their hands upon the sick, and pray for healing. The celebration of the sacraments in Pentecostal worship is an opportunity to invite the saints of God once again to the altar to encounter the Holy Spirit in the celebration of water baptism, the Lord's Supper, foot-washing, and the laying on of hands. Each sacrament directly corresponds to the redemptive work of the Holy Trinity. In this regard, *the sacraments are an ongoing altar call in which the believer encounters God in Christ and through the Holy Spirit.* Just as the Spirit animates Pentecostal worship in inspired preaching, anointed singing, joyful shouts of praise, and dancing, the Spirit also animates the sacraments. When believers experience water baptism, the Lord's Supper, or foot-washing, they encounter Christ's priestly ministry through the Spirit of grace. When the sick call for prayer, holy hands anoint the sick with oil and the Spirit is present. Through the Holy Spirit, worshipers transcend time and space as they share sacramental experiences with Christ and the redeemed community. When believers enter the baptismal water and are baptized into Christ, they share in His personal baptism in the Jordan River. When believers gather at the Lord's Table to share bread and wine – the body and blood of Jesus – they join with the Lord and all believers of the past who have received bread and wine, and all those in the future who will receive bread and wine. When believers take the towel and basin to wash the feet of another, it is because they have been baptized into Christ and are participants in Christ's reconciling and sanctifying work. Through Christ the High Priest and the Spirit of grace, sacraments are more than mere reenactments or memorials to God's redemptive acts. The baptismal water, the towel and basin, the bread and wine, and the anointing oil become mediatory gifts. In Christ and the Spirit, celebration of the sacraments becomes participation in God's redemptive acts. Worship becomes an expression of ongoing saving faith.

The challenge for Pentecostals is, "How can the celebration of sacraments enrich Pentecostal worship?" This is not a call for the establishment of a formal Pentecostal liturgy, nor is it a suggestion to diminish spontaneity or "Spirit movement" in Pentecostal worship. The Holy Spirit is utterly free. The Spirit cannot be domesticated, manipulated, or institutionalized. The Spirit cannot be confined to an established liturgy. Pentecostals should understand that the freedom of the Spirit means that the Spirit is free to act as a mediator of grace in sacraments. Some Pentecostals have been critical of liturgical ritualism, but have failed to discern that enthusiastic worship can also miss the movements of the Spirit. A proper celebration of the sacraments offers worshipers the opportunity to be properly positioned and ordered so that the Spirit can be encountered and discerned. The sacraments originate in the Spirit-empowered ministry of Jesus Christ. The intent here is to suggest ways sacraments can be fully appreciated in Pentecostal spirituality. The Spirit's movement in and through the sacraments sanctifies and transforms the worshiping community.

3

THE ANOINTED TOUCH

ANOINTING WITH OIL
AND LAYING ON HANDS

> Is anyone among you sick? Then he must call for the elders
> of the church and they are to pray over him, anointing him
> with oil in the name of the Lord; and the prayer offered in
> faith will restore the one who is sick, and the Lord will
> raise him up, and if he has committed sins, they will be
> forgiven him (James 5:14-15).

Since the earliest days of the movement Pentecostals have prayed
for the sick. The practice of anointing with oil and laying on hands
is an excellent example of the embodied spirituality and
sacramental nature of Pentecostalism and serves as a model for
understanding pentecostal sacraments. The periodicals of early
Pentecostalism are filled with testimonies of healing.

> Sister Lemon of Whittier, who had been a sufferer for
> eighteen years and could receive no help from physicians,
> and had been bed-ridden for fourteen years of that time
> has been marvelously healed by the Lord through the
> laying on of hands and the prayer of faith. She has been
> walking to meetings. The opposers of the work cannot
> deny that a notable miracle has been performed through
> the mighty name of Jesus (AF, Nov 1906).

Pentecostal spirituality is a physical spirituality. The Holy Spirit
dwells within the believer; the Spirit fills the believer, and the
believer often expresses these divine encounters with physical
manifestations—dancing, shouting, clapping, and tongues-speech.

When Pentecostals pray for the sick, it is often expressed in the physical act of anointing the sick with oil and/or laying hands on the sick. The oil represents the presence and anointing of the Holy Spirit. Spirit-filled believers are laying on "holy hands." Sometimes handkerchiefs are anointed with oil and these "anointed cloths" are sent to the sick. In divine healing, the Spirit touches the body and effects physical healing. Healing is a sensory experience. The body is healed and all pain associated with the injury or disease ceases. The healed person *feels* better. This sacramental practice involves fellowship with Christ and Spirit in the church, and the interaction between that which is spiritual and that which is physical.

In the Scriptures, anointing with oil and the laying on of hands are not always associated together. Throughout the Acts of the Apostles, there are many examples where apostles and elders laid their hands upon believers for healing and reception of the Holy Spirit, but anointing with oil is not mentioned. It may be that in the primitive church anointing with oil was so associated with the laying on of hands that Luke did not find it necessary to mention. However, it is certain that anointing with oil suggests some kind of touch. For the purposes of our discussion, we will assume that anointing with oil and the laying on of hands are related expressions of one sacramental rite—***the anointed touch***.

THE ANOINTED TOUCH
IN THE MINISTRY OF JESUS

The title *Christ* means "anointed one." After Jesus was baptized in the Jordan River and the Spirit of God descended upon Him, He declared, "The Spirit of the Lord is upon Me, because He anointed Me to preach the gospel to the poor. He has sent me to proclaim release to the captives, and recovery of sight to the blind, to set free those who are oppressed, to proclaim the favorable year of the Lord" (Luke 4:18-19). The Holy Spirit empowered Jesus for ministry. But why would Jesus, who is the eternal Son, consubstantial with the Father and the Spirit, need to be empowered for ministry? Paul wrote that Jesus "existed in the form of God . . . but emptied Himself" (Philip. 2:6-7). In the Incarnation, the eternal Son "emptied Himself" of divine power and authority, but never ceased to be consubstantial with the Father and the Spirit. In Jesus Christ, we have the perfect union of full divinity and full humanity. So then, if Jesus "emptied Himself," how did He perform His ministry of miracles and deliverance? Luke answers that Jesus was "full of the Holy Spirit" (Luke 4:1) and went forth "in the power of the Spirit" (Luke 4:1, 14). The author of Hebrews, quoting Isaiah, associates the anointing of the Spirit upon Jesus with the "oil of gladness" (Is. 61:1-3; Heb. 1:9; cf. Ps. 45:7). The "oil of gladness" is God's remedy for the "mourning" and suffering of God's people. Because Jesus is anointed with the "oil of gladness," God's people can be redeemed, healed, and comforted. The sounds of suffering are replaced by the sounds of joy. When Jesus, the Anointed One, entered Jerusalem on Palm Sunday, He was greeted with the sounds of celebration: "Hosanna! Blessed is He who comes in the name of the Lord" (Mark 11:9).

Throughout the Gospels, Jesus' anointed touch transformed the lives of the suffering. A. J. Gordon wrote that Jesus is a person "in whom an abounding infectious health is present, so that it only needs the contact of a finger-tip that it may leap like the electric current to thrill and vitalize the sickly body" (LRE, May 1909). The anointed touch of Jesus cleansed lepers, cooled fevers, restored sight to the blind, comforted the fearful, healed deaf ears, blessed children, strengthened the crippled, and raised the dead. Because of the power of His touch, people reached out to touch Him, or His garments, and were healed. Jesus allowed even sinners to touch Him. After His resurrection, Jesus implored His doubting and fearful disciples, "See My hands and My feet, that it is I Myself; *touch Me and see*" (Luke 24:39). Just before He ascended to Heaven, Jesus "lifted up His hands and blessed" His disciples in anticipation of Pentecost (Luke 24:49-50).

Jesus Christ is "the Anointed One." Anointed by the Holy Spirit, Jesus went forth "in the power of the Spirit." It is clear that the saving and healing power of Jesus—the anointing—was transferred to the suffering through His anointed touch. In some cases, Jesus is active—He reaches out to touch the suffering individual. In other cases, Jesus is somewhat passive—as He walks by, those who are suffering reach out to touch him, or his clothes. In all cases, there is a perceivable and physical transfer of power, and people are healed and delivered (Mark 5:30; Luke 6:19; 8:46). The Gospels insist "that Jesus' body was a source of power which could be released physically, through a touch accompanied by faith" (Tipei, *The Laying on of Hands in the New Testament*, 2009). Even unbelievers were made to wonder at the miracles performed with the hands of Jesus (Mark 6:2).

THE ANOINTED TOUCH
IN THE APOSTOLIC CHURCH

All of the Gospels tell of Jesus commissioning His disciples to continue His redemptive work. The commissioning of the disciples involves divine empowerment. In the Gospel of John, the Holy Spirit is given at the bequest of the Son. Jesus is "the way, and the truth, and the life," and the Spirit is the teacher of truth (John 14:6; 14:26; 16:7, 13-14). One of the primary works of the Spirit in the world is to "convict the world concerning sin . . . because they do not believe" in Jesus Christ. The Spirit's work also includes the declaration of righteousness and judgment (John 16:8-11). After the resurrection, Jesus "breathed on them and said to them, 'Receive the Holy Spirit. If you forgive the sins of any, their sins have been forgiven them; if you retain the sins of any, they have been retained'" (John 20:22-23). Just as God breathed life into Adam, Jesus Christ bestowed the breath of God—the Holy Spirit— upon and into His disciples. With the bestowal of the Holy Spirit, the disciples are given the authority to declare the forgiveness of sin, and also judgment upon those who do not believe.

In Matthew, Jesus said, "All authority has been given to Me in heaven and on earth. Go therefore . . ." (Matt. 28:18-19). Jesus' authority transcends that of the ancient scribal tradition, and even that of Moses. He challenged the authority of the scribal tradition with the words, "I say to you . . ." (Matt. 5:18-44). He is the enfleshed fulfillment of the Torah and the Prophets (Matt. 5:17). Jesus has authority to forgive sin, to heal all manner of disease, and subdue the power of demons. Also, He has authority over the created order (Matt. 14:22-33). His authority was challenged by the chief priests and elders of Israel and mocked by the Roman authorities. Even the condemned criminals who were dying with Him mocked Jesus (Matt. 21:23; 27:27-31, 39-44). But the resurrected Jesus is vindicated by the Father and has been given all authority "in heaven and earth." Jesus grants authority to His disciples so that His redemptive mission may continue to all the nations. They have been given "authority over unclean spirits" and commissioned to "heal the sick, raise the dead, cleanse the lepers, cast out demons" (Matt. 10:1-8). They are to "make disciples" by teaching and baptizing. As they do, they will often find that their authority will be questioned and mocked. With the grant of His divine authority, Jesus also assures His disciples of His presence to "the end of the age" (Matt. 28:20).

The apostolic practice of anointing the sick with oil is first mentioned in the Gospel of Mark:

> And He summoned the twelve and began to send them out in pairs, and gave them authority over the unclean spirits . . . They went out and preached that men should repent. And they were casting out many demons and *were anointing with oil many sick people and healing them* (Mark 6:7-13).

In Luke's story of the Good Samaritan, the Samaritan uses oil to treat the wounds of his patient (Luke 10:34). This is testimony to the ancient practice of using oil as a medicine. However, Mark's account of the apostolic practice of anointing with oil is different. It reflects the Old Testament tradition that oil is often associated with the endowment of the Holy Spirit (1 Samuel 16:13; Psalm 89:20; Isaiah 61:1).

The use of oil in Mark is associated with miraculous healing and the anointing of the Holy Spirit. The transference of power and authority through the anointed touch was normative in the apostolic church. Mark records Jesus' commissioning of His disciples in terms of charismatic manifestations and miraculous signs: "These signs will accompany those who have believed: in My name they will cast out demons, they will speak with new tongues; they will pick up serpents, and if they drink any deadly poison, it will not hurt them; they will lay hands on the sick, and they will recover" (Mark 16:17-18). This seems somewhat unusual because Jesus laments that the unbelieving generation is seeking signs, and he warns of the signs and wonders of false prophets (Mark 8:11-12; 13:22). However, the words of Mark 16:17-20 correspond with the apostolic commission of Mark 6:7-13. The disciples are given authority over "unclean spirits," they are commissioned to preach, and the sick are healed. In both texts, charismatic signs are the confirmation of the preached word (Mark 16:20).

Luke offers two accounts. First, in the Gospel, Jesus tells the disciples that they will receive "the promise of My Father" and be "clothed with power from on high." He then lifts His hands to bless them (Luke 24:49-50). Then in Acts, Jesus said, "but you will receive power when the Holy Spirit has come upon you" (Acts 1:8). As Jesus ascended into Heaven, the "Anointed One" bestowed the "Anointing." The church, as the body of Christ, is empowered with the anointed touch of Jesus. Jesus' ministry of healing and salvation is continued through His anointed disciples. The transfer of anointing has its precedent in the Old Testament. Moses transferred his prophetic anointing to his successor, Joshua. "Now Joshua the son of Nun was filled with the spirit of wisdom, for Moses had laid his hands on him" (Deut. 34:9). When Jesus lifted His hands to bless His disciples, He was acting in the Mosaic tradition. Also, Elisha received the prophetic mantle of his mentor, Elijah (2 Kings 2:9-22). Elisha had requested that "a double portion" of Elijah's spirit be bestowed upon him. As Elijah was being taken up to Heaven in a fiery chariot, his mantle (garment, or robe) fell so that Elisha received it. When Jesus told the disciples they would be "clothed with power from on high," He was drawing from the Elisha tradition. But even more significant is the promise of Joel 2:28: "I will pour out My Spirit on all mankind." Jesus is "sending forth the promise of the Father." In the words of the Pentecostal "full gospel"—Jesus is the Holy Spirit baptizer. Because of the Spirit's presence and empowerment, "at the hands of the apostles many signs and wonders were taking place among the people" (Acts 5:12). The anointed hands of the apostles have become the sacramental presence of the Anointed One—Jesus Christ.

The anointed touch in Acts is often associated with reception of the Spirit. Peter and John prayed for the Samaritan believers to receive the Spirit. "Then they began laying their hands on them, and they were receiving the Holy Spirit" (Acts 8:17). Saul was healed of blindness and filled with the Spirit as Ananias laid his hand on him (Acts 9:17). The believers at Ephesus received the Spirit as Paul "laid his hands upon them" (Acts 19:6). The anointed touch was also employed in commissioning various ministries in the church. The apostles commissioned the first deacons, "after praying, they laid their hands on them" (Acts 6:6). When Barnabas and Saul were commissioned as apostles, the leaders of the church "prayed and laid their hands on them" and "sent them away" (Acts 13:3). Timothy received his pastoral call "through prophetic utterance with the laying on of hands by the presbytery" (1 Tim. 4:14). This is not to imply that reception of the Holy Spirit, or the spiritual gifts, requires the laying on of hands. Just as there are many instances when healings occurred without the anointed touch, there are also instances when the Holy Spirit was received without the anointed touch. So then, what is the purpose of the anointed touch in relation to reception of the Holy Spirit and confirmation of ministry? Remember, Luke tells us that just before Jesus ascended, He told His disciples of the promise of the Spirit and "He lifted up His hands and blessed them" (Luke 24:40). The gesture of lifting His hands corresponds to the promise of the Spirit. The blessing of Christ is the gift of the Holy Spirit. The transfer of anointing is implied and it expresses the continuity of Christ's presence with

His disciples. Christ blessed His church with lifted hands. The church has become the healing hands of Christ extended to the world, and through the hands of His anointed servants, signs and wonders are performed (Acts 4:30; 5:12). The lifted hands and blessing of the Anointed One are expressed throughout Acts with the anointed touch of Spirit-filled believers.

The anointed touch is also associated with prayer for the sick. It is implied in the healing of the lame man at the Beautiful Gate. Luke records that Peter "took him by the right hand and lifted him up" (Acts 3:7 NKJV). This is more than a helpful gesture. Peter, Spirit-filled and anointed, extended his hand to the lame man and "lifted him up." The healing of "his feet and ankles" corresponds to Peter's extended hand—the anointed touch. On the island of Malta, the shipwrecked Paul prayed for the father of Publius, who was afflicted with a fever and dysentery. "Paul went in to see him and after he had prayed, he laid his hands on him and healed him" (Acts 28:8). Many others on the island came to Paul to receive healing through the anointed touch. Furthermore, just as many were healed as they touched the garments of Jesus, in Acts we discover that the sick were carried into the streets and healed as Peter's shadow fell upon them (Acts 5:14-16). Also, handkerchiefs or aprons were carried from the body of Paul to the sick "and the diseases left them and the evil spirits went out" (Acts 19:11-12).

The anointed touch in James 5:14-15 reflects the apostolic practice in the writings of Mark and Luke. James wrote, "The prayer offered in faith will *restore* the one who is sick, and the Lord will *raise* him up." So, what is James telling us about the significance of the anointed touch? James, following the example of his Lord, is addressing more than healing; he is also speaking about the forgiveness of sin (Mark 2:3-12), and resurrection from the dead. Salvation is holistic, that is, God desires that the whole person—body, soul, spirit—be touched by God's saving power. Salvation is healing—being healed from the corruption and disease of sin. Ultimately, salvation is resurrection and glorification — deliverance from the corruption of this present age. James understands the anointed touch as signifying salvation in a broader sense. Is James speaking about a sacramental act of healing? Yes. He wrote,   ". . . pray for one another so that you may be healed." Sick people often die. It seems that James is considering that possibility. So then, what is the significance of the anointed touch when the sick are not healed? Their sins are forgiven and they shall be saved, that is, *raised up to new life*. In other words, the sick may die, but those who die in Christ are confident in the resurrection. Paul declared, "But if the Spirit of Him who raised Jesus from the dead dwells in you, He who raised Christ Jesus from the dead will also give life to your mortal bodies through His Spirit who dwells in you" (Rom. 8:11).

The sick person calls for the "elders of the church." This suggests that the sick believer is too sick to travel, possibly close to death. So, the church responds to the call and comes together with the sick believer. The sick believer is to be "anointed with oil," which signifies the presence of the Holy Spirit, in "the name of the Lord" — Jesus Christ. The church gathered together is to offer the prayer of faith. The sick person calling for the elders of the church is an act of faith. The elders' anointed touch "is the visible confession of confidence in the power of Christ to make whole" (LRE, May 1909). James presents the gathered church, sick and well, in fellowship with the Holy Trinity. The Son and the Spirit are present as the two hands of the Father. The praying church is a community of healing and care which is expressed in the anointed touch and becomes a sacramental means of grace to the suffering.

The power and authority of the church is wholly derived from Christ and the Spirit—the Anointed One and the Anointing. The power and authority of Jesus is unique. Because of the intra-Trinitarian relationship between the Son and the Spirit, Christ is anointed by the Spirit in a unique manner that cannot be shared. The elders of the church represent those who are anointed, that is "full of the Spirit and of wisdom" and "righteous" (Acts 6:33; James 5:16). Because of the healing powers associated with the apostles and elders of the apostolic church, many pagans believed them to be gods (Acts 14:11-13). But James likens the elders to the prophet Elijah who "was a man with a nature like ours" (James 5:17). In other words, the elders of the church are not divine. However, in relationship with Christ, believers may be filled with the Holy Spirit and anointed for ministry. As believers exercised the anointed touch in the apostolic church, they were acting as "petitioners and mediators of divine power" (Tipei). Anointed believers act "in the name of Jesus" and in the power of the Holy Spirit. Further, there is no intrinsic power in the various media used in healing—Peter's shadow, Paul's handkerchiefs, or anointing oil. The healing power always proceeds from God. God is free to use various substances as symbols of God's power, and even to use them as a medium, or channel, to transfer God's power. Therefore, the prayer of faith and the anointed touch are sacramental means of grace. Through the prayers of anointed and faithful believers the presence of Christ and the Spirit is manifested and those who are suffering are comforted, healed, and made confident in the hope of the resurrection. "The effective prayer of a righteous man can accomplish much" (James 5:16). Healing and salvation are two aspects of the same divine work. Salvation is the healing of sin and its corrupting effects on the body.

A PENTECOSTAL SACRAMENT

The proclamation that "Jesus is our Healer" is essential to the Pentecostal *way of salvation* (Isaiah 53:4-5; 1 Peter 2:24). The Pentecostal doctrine of divine healing in the Atonement is not a novel concept—it faithfully represents the teaching of the early church. Jesus is savior and the Great Physician. W. J. Seymour wrote, "Sickness and disease are destroyed through the precious atonement of Jesus . . . a body that knew no sin and disease was given for these imperfect bodies of ours" (AF, Sep 1906). "Through Jesus, we are entitled to health and sanctification of the soul and body" (AF, Dec 1906). W. C. Stevens proclaimed that "Christ's vicarious assumption of human sickness is the same as that employed in the case of sins." He explained:

While our mortal life contracts disease, Jesus' life banishes disease. Contagious disease is dangerous to us, but the life of Jesus is destructive to disease. The very life of Jesus is of healing virtue. It is immortality touching mortality with a foretaste of the coming redemption. No child of God can afford to be living in mortality without these sippings of the life to come. The experience of the Spirit's quickening in our mortal flesh brings literal bodily immortality nigh to our consciousness and it puts us in advance touch with "the power of the age to come" (PE, 23 Aug 1924).

Alex Boddy wrote that believers may have "divine health" through union with the "life-giving Christ" and the Holy Spirit who is "the indwelling Divine Life." "If any man is in Christ he is a new creation — the old nature passes away, all things become new. We believe that this is true of the body as well as of the soul" (*Confidence*, Aug 1910). Throughout his writings Boddy says, "the oil follows the blood," that is, Pentecost follows Calvary. He wrote,

> The outpouring of the Blood at Calvary (together with the Resurrection) is the preparation for a true "Pentecost" for each one. The Blood of Jesus Christ, God's Son, cleanses us from all sin. Then the Holy Ghost is glad to come, and free to come. He comes (1) as the Holy Anointing OIL from above (I John ii., 20-27); (2) As the Presence which is as a Consuming FIRE (Heb. xii., 29) burning up all the chaff. (Jesus baptizes with the Holy Ghost and with Fire – Matt. iii., 11). Then He also comes as Living WATER, now that Jesus is glorified (John vii., 35). Out of the Spirit-baptized shall flow rivers of Living Water. Hallelujah! (*Confidence*, Aug 1911).

The healing of the body is a blessing of sanctification. "A sanctified body is one in perfect health, through faith in God. It does not mean we could not get sick, but we are maintained in health by faith" (AF, Jan 1907). Although all sickness is a result of the corruption of sin, the sickness of a saint should not be interpreted as evidence of willful disobedience. After all, Job was blameless, but suffered (COGE, 11 Jul 1914). Some Pentecostals taught that Christians should trust God with healing, and therefore faithful believers would not use medicine. What was the "divine prescription" for the sick? "Jesus is all the medicine you need." How do believers receive divine healing? "James gives us explicit directions as to what we should do when we get sick (James 5:14)" (COGE, 15 Apr 1910). Will all believers be healed? Yes, said some Pentecostals, suggesting that failure to receive healing was a sign of weak faith. But others offered a more biblically balanced perspective. One pastor wrote that "in every case of sickness we can come to Jesus . . . the redemption of our body is already completed by the death and resurrection of Jesus, but the full redemption of our body can only become our possession when our Savior comes again" (*Confidence*, Apr 1915). The healing of the body is a sign that anticipates the resurrection of the body. Most Pentecostals believe that "living in the fullness of God" is more important than divine health for the body (COGE, 3 Feb 1917). Many believers testified to receiving the baptism in the Holy Spirit as they sought to be healed.

The practice of praying for the sick by anointing with oil and laying on hands has been central to Pentecostal faith and practice. In an early letter, A. J. Tomlinson wrote,

> Hundreds have received the Baptism with the Holy Ghost and spoken in tongues as they did on the day of Pentecost . . . when the altar calls were made hundreds and even thousands were moved by the Spirit to seek salvation or the Baptism with the Holy Ghost. Streaks of fire have been witnessed by observers. Wonderful demonstrations of the Spirit in many different ways [sic]. *I am not able to tell the numbers that have received healing for their bodies as* we anointed them with oil, prayed for and laid our hands on them (*Church of God Publications* 1901-1923 DVD).

Pentecostals proclaimed "the full gospel." For early Pentecostals, the anointed touch was essential because it was "the Bible way." It occurred with great frequency in Pentecostal worship services and camp meetings. Early Pentecostal periodicals are filled with the testimonies of the faithful who were healed in the name of Jesus through the means of the anointed touch.

Early Pentecostal sacramental teaching followed the Protestant model of two (or three) sacraments. Most early Pentecostal creeds listed the "ordinances" or "sacraments" of the church as water baptism and the Lord's Supper. Many included foot-washing. Because most early Pentecostals were anti-Catholic and anti-liturgical, it did not occur to them to view anointing and laying on of hands as a formal sacrament of the church. However, in faith and practice the anointed touch was a prevalent Pentecostal sacrament. Many early Pentecostal creeds included prayer for the sick by anointing and laying on of hands in connection with an affirmation of divine healing. The first issue of *The Apostolic Faith* listed the teachings of W. J. Seymour and the Apostolic Faith Movement (AF, Sep 1906). The teachings include the three Pentecostal works of grace—justification, sanctification, and baptism in the Holy Spirit—and "seeking healing." Among the Scripture references to support the doctrine of healing are, Mark 16:16-18 and James 5:14. Both of these passages prescribe laying on hands in offering prayer for the sick. The earliest creedal statement of the Church of God (Cleveland, Tennessee) offers a list of "teachings that are made prominent" with accompanying Scriptural citations (COGE, 15 Aug 1910). The sacramental teachings include:

- Water baptism by immersion—Matt. 28:19; Mark 1:9-10; John 3:22-23; Acts 8:36-38.

- Divine Healing Provided for All in the Atonement— Ps 103:3; Isaiah 53:4-5; Matt. 8:17; Jas 5:14-16; 1 Pet 2:24.

- The Lord's Supper—Luke 22:17-20; 1 Cor. 11:23-33.

- Washing the Saints' Feet—John 13:4-17; 1 Tim. 5:9-10.

Again, James 5:14-15 is given in support of the doctrine of divine healing. The anointed touch is essential to the doctrine of divine healing. The Pentecostal "full gospel" includes all sacramental practices that were blessed by Christ and practiced by the apostles. This sacramental practice was a sign that the Pentecostal church was a restoration of apostolic faith. George Holmes expressed the Pentecostal view of the anointed touch when he wrote, "This ordinance to the Church is surely as binding as those of Communion and baptism. If it were not God's intention to heal, this ordinance would be superfluous" (PE, 19 Jul 1959).

In the New Testament, the Spirit-anointed elders were charged with praying for the sick. In the early church, only baptized believers were permitted to anoint the sick because it was expected that they received the Spirit at baptism. Likewise, early Pentecostals believed that Spirit-baptized believers are a "channel through which the Spirit may operate to do the works of Jesus Christ" (COGE, 11 May 1918). This expresses the sacramental nature which is essential to Pentecostal spirituality. The church is a visible and physical expression of the extended hands of Jesus Christ to those who are suffering.

Early Pentecostals were sacramental, and when it was considered to be "the Bible way," they could even be somewhat liturgical. Because of their sincere desire to be apostolic in faith and practice, proper biblical order was important. But proper biblical order always meant the presence of the Holy Spirit. The Church of God *Book of Doctrines* offered the usual manner by which the anointed touch was administered:

> The sick one calls upon the elders of the church to pray for his healing. (The elders in this case are considered any that are leaders in the church service — faithful brethren or sisters.) They anoint with oil (usually olive oil), by dropping a few drops from a bottle on the head of the sick one. This is done with the prayer of faith. Frequently, the evil spirit must be rebuked from the sick one's body—just as in Matthew 8:28-34 out of whom Jesus cast the evil spirits—and then deliverance comes. Oftentimes the evil spirit is rebuked by the Holy Ghost in unknown tongues.

The anointed touch is presented as a charismatic sacrament in which Holy Spirit is present and often speaks. Also, just as the early church exorcised demons with the baptismal anointing, Pentecostals often rebuked evil spirits that might be the cause of disease. This is a form of godliness in which the power of God is affirmed and demonstrated in physical manifestations, including a healed body.

Alex Boddy published a "form of procedure" for administering the anointed touch. He wrote, "Pouring a few drops of olive oil into his left palm, the Elder prays that God will graciously sanctify the oil: and that He will use it as a channel of spiritual blessing to the sufferer for Christ's sake, also as a symbol of consecration to His blessed service, and a token of the coming of the Holy Ghost" (*Confidence*, Apr-Jun 1921). Boddy presents the anointed touch in a sacramental manner that is reminiscent of the early church. Through the prayer of the elder, the oil is to be sanctified by the Spirit of grace and becomes "a channel of spiritual blessing." The anointing oil is touched by the divine Anointing. The oil signifies the participation of the Holy Spirit. Not only could anointed men and women be channels of God's grace, but anointed oil was a "means of grace" as well. Pentecostals have always associated the Holy Spirit with oil. Boddy declared,

> "He anointeth my head with oil, my cup runneth over." The oil of the Holy Ghost is poured upon our heads, and when we get filled, it will run over, that we may help others . . . when the oil of the Holy Ghost overflows, it will saturate and thrill and fill with the power of God other souls (AF, Sep 1907).

The baptism of the Holy Spirit is "the Holy Anointing Oil" from above (*Confidence*, Aug 1911). The church, which is the body of Christ, must be anointed with "the blessed oil of the Holy Ghost" (COGE, 21 Feb 1920). Donald Gee wrote that the Pentecostal church is "well lubricated" by the oil of the Spirit. He exclaimed, "I bless God for the oil. Hallelujah for the Oil!" (PE, 17 Aug 1935).

The anointed handkerchief was another "means of grace" by which the sick may be healed. Oil was often used to anoint handkerchiefs so that they could be sent to the sick. Sometimes, sick individuals would send a handkerchief to the church to be anointed and returned. This practice was common among Pentecostals from Azusa Street in Los Angeles to those in the Appalachian Mountains of Tennessee and North Carolina, and throughout the world. W. J. Seymour offered an early report from the Azusa St. revival:

> The Lord is graciously healing many sick bodies. People are healed at the Mission almost every day. Requests come in for prayer from all over. They are presented in the meeting and the Spirit witnesses in many cases that prayer is answered, and when we hear from them they are healed. Handkerchiefs are sent in to be blest, and are returned to the sick and they are healed in many cases. One day nine handkerchiefs were blest, another day sixteen. A man came with a broken arm and was healed. The mission people never take medicine. They do not want it. They have taken Jesus for their healer and He always heals (AF, Jan 1907).

This practice was a sign of the restoration of the apostolic church (AF, May 1907). A. J. Tomlinson reported that Pentecostals were "practicing the Bible way of healing." He continued:

> The common way now is by sending request by wire and letter, and by sending handkerchiefs and aprons. We pray for the sick every day, but on Sunday about 12:30 we have from twenty to forty handkerchiefs to pray over besides a number of requests. When this time comes we spread the handkerchiefs out on the altar and the saints gather around and prayers are offered up in the earnestness of our souls. We are often reminded of the experience of the apostles . . . We think of every handkerchief representing a sick person . . . And oh, how the saints pray! Then, as we cannot get to the people and anoint them and lay our hands on them we lay our hands on the handkerchiefs and anoint them and send them to be placed on the sick ones. Many have sent us good news of instantaneous healing when the handkerchief touched the body, while others have stated that they began

to amend that very hour. And either way God gets the glory (COGE, 10 Jun 1922).

There have been hundreds of healing testimonies printed in various Pentecostal publications. Here I will offer just two of the "good reports" that were printed in the *Church of God Evangel*. Sister Mary Davis wrote:

> I am still praising God for healing in my body. I was very low and Sister Blake sent my handkerchief to Brother Tomlinson for the saints there to pray over and anoint with oil in the name of Jesus. When the handkerchief returned I was completely healed of consumption. Glory to God forever (COGE, 26 Nov 1921).

Sister Laura Williams said:

> I want to testify of His wonderful healing power. I had a large growth on my head for twenty-seven years and last winter it hurt so bad that I asked the good Lord to heal my head. About the middle of February it burst and commenced running very bad. So in July I sent a handkerchief to Brother Tomlinson, for him and the saints to pray over it anointing it with oil. When it came back I wore it on my head for a few nights and the place was healed wonderfully. I thank and praise the Lord for it (COGE, 31 Dec 1921).

Did early Pentecostals believe that healing grace was transferred through the anointed touch? Can the anointed human hand, anointed oil, or an anointed handkerchief be a channel through which the power of God touches and heals the sick? The primary concern of Pentecostal theology is that every believer can have a direct and unmediated encounter with Christ and the Spirit. W. J. Seymour insisted, "We are not divine healers any more than we are divine saviors. Healing is done through Almighty God" (AF, Oct 1906). Concerning the anointing oil, J. T. Butlin wrote, "There is no healing power in the oil itself, and if a patient thinks too much of the oil as a means of healing, he will be disappointed. It is the Lord who heals" (PE, 23 Aug 1924). These Pentecostals were adamant that divine healing is provided in the atonement of Jesus Christ and through the power of the Holy Spirit. Also, they were utterly committed to obedience to the Holy Scriptures. As we have observed, Pentecostal spirituality is often manifested in physical actions. Yes, divine healing is the saving work of Christ and Spirit; but it also involves the "prayer of faith" and the anointed touch. Pentecostals understand that healing often occurs due to the anointed prayers and faith of Spirit-filled believers, even when the recipient of healing grace is incapable of faith. Faith is a gift of the Spirit of grace who is ever-present within the believing community.

Sacraments are charismatic in that they require the direct mediation of Christ and presence of the Spirit. For Pentecostals, sacraments are efficacious when they are observed in faithful obedience to the Scriptures by the sanctified church where Christ and the Spirit are present. This spirituality represents the Father (the Anointer) embracing humanity, and all creation, with His two hands — Christ (the Anointed One) and Spirit (the Anointing). The Word became flesh. The Spirit is poured out upon all flesh. Flesh is of the created order. Jesus Christ is the perfect union of humanity and divinity. The Spirit baptizes and anoints all who are in Christ. Also, the Spirit moves and rests upon all creation. Therefore, saving and healing grace can be conveyed in the waters of baptism and foot-washing, through the bread and cup of Holy Communion, and through anointed hands, oil, and handkerchiefs.

An early Pentecostal, Maggie Geddis, testified, "I simply obeyed the dictates of the Holy Spirit. Glory to God. It was no longer I but He. The power seemed to center in my hands, and I promised God I would obey Him in the future and lay hands on the sick, whenever and wherever He sent me" (AP). Humans in Christ and filled with the Holy Spirit can become a sacramental presence, mediators of the Spirit of grace. In becoming "partakers of the divine nature" (2 Peter 1:4), humans also become participants in the transference of divine grace. The church, as the gathered people of God, is a sacramental presence in the world. Also, a single person, created in the image of God and reborn by the Spirit, can be a sacramental presence. When a pastor or church elder walks into a hospital room to pray for the sick, they become a means of grace to the suffering. Men and women who are anointed by the Holy Spirit are collaborators with gracious activity of the Spirit.

THE GIFT OF GOD

Once, I was watching a prominent Charismatic evangelist on a Christian network preach a message on salvation and healing. As he preached, I listened attentively. I thought, *He's really doing a good job presenting the gospel.* Then, he gave the altar call. He said, "If you're ready to receive from God, come now and sow your $1000 seed faith gift into our ministry." I wish I could say that I was surprised, but I was not. This is all too common in contemporary Pentecostal and Charismatic churches. And frankly, it is appalling. Salvation and healing are the *free* gifts of God. Jesus paid it all!

Simon Magus was a notorious Samaritan magician who heard the preaching of Philip, believed on Christ and was baptized (Acts 8:13). Because of his pre-conversion experience in the magical arts, he was "constantly amazed" at the "signs and great miracles" that were taking place at the hands of the apostles and elders of the church. He was seduced by power and offered money to the apostles so that he might receive the power of the Spirit. Peter's rebuke was harsh. "May your silver perish with you." Previously, Peter had pronounced judgment upon Ananias and Sapphira because they had lied to the Holy Spirit (Acts 5). They died at the feet of Peter. Simon was offered the possibility of repentance, but was sternly warned of impending eternal destruction. Peter declared, "Your heart is not right before God."

Jesus warned of the corrupting influence of power and money: "No one can serve two masters; for either he will hate the one and love the other, or he will be devoted to one and despise the other. You cannot serve God and wealth" (Matt. 6:24). Likewise, Paul said that leaders in the church should be "free from the love of money" (1 Tim. 3:3). He explained, "For the love of money is a root of all sorts of evil, and some by longing for it have wandered away from the faith and pierced themselves with many griefs" (1 Tim. 6:10).

Just as Peter had discerned the greed of Ananias' heart, he discerned the "intent" of Simon's heart. Simon Magus' love of power and money had produced in him "the gall of bitterness" and "the bondage of iniquity." Indeed, he had wandered from the faith. In the tradition of the church, Simon is remembered as the first heretic. Also, his name is associated with the scandal of power and greed within the church. The crime of "simony" is defined as buying the holy offices of the church. Simon was not the last believer to be scandalized by the love of money.

In 1517, Pope Leo X offered indulgences, a pardon of temporal punishment, to all who would give money in support of the construction of St. Peter's Basilica. To put this in the language of the contemporary Pentecostal Movement, if believers would "plant a seed faith gift" in support of St. Peter's, then their sins would be forgiven. In effect, God's grace was for sale. Johann Tetzel, a German Dominican friar, was appointed commissioner for the Pope and authorized to sell indulgences throughout Germany. Tetzel preached, ". . . all who confess and in penance put alms into the coffer according to the counsel of the confessor, will obtain complete remission of all their sins." Like a wolf, Tetzel preyed upon the despair of God's lambs, enriching himself as well as the coffers of the Pope. It was Tetzel's activity that stirred the passions of Martin Luther. Luther denounced the practice of selling indulgences. He wrote, "It is certain that when the penny jingles into the money-box, gain and avarice can be increased, but the result of the intercession of the Church is in the power of God alone." According to Luther, salvation, and pardon from sin, could not be purchased because "the just shall live by faith." Salvation and healing are the free and gracious acts of God. With Luther's protest, the Protestant Reformation was launched. The Roman

Catholic Church eventually recognized the error. After the Council of Trent, Pope Pius V issued a decree that forbade the granting of indulgences associated with any financial transaction.

The Pentecostal Movement has been scandalized by the "prosperity gospel." The love of money has corrupted Pentecostal and Charismatic churches from pulpit to pew. It seems that the new sacramental element is coin and currency. A relationship with God is presented in terms of a contractual agreement between business partners. The anointing and grace of God have become commodities that are auctioned to the highest bidder. Charismatic men and women who proclaim the message of Jesus Christ have cheapened that which is more desirable than the finest gold. In the process, their anointing has become "a ring of gold in a swine's snout" (Proverbs 11:22). It may be that, like Simon Magus, the Pentecostal Movement will perish with its silver.

This much is certain. The substance of the kingdom of God is not the perishable wealth of this present age. The gift of God cannot be obtained with money. The price of human redemption has been paid with the blood of God's dear Son. God the Father has extended his two hands — Son and Spirit — to save and heal all who will respond in sincere faith. Rich and poor alike have the same access to the throne of grace. Luther was right. The righteous by faith shall live!

Pentecostals have been praying for the sick since the beginning of the movement. There have been many testimonies of miraculous healings. But, not all have been healed. Many have continued to suffer and eventually succumb to the disease that afflicted them. Among Pentecostals, there has existed a tension between the "prayer of faith" for the sick and the fact that many have died in spite of the faithful prayers of the saints.

Here we must return to the earlier exposition of James 5:14-15. Remember, James speaks of the anointed touch in terms of the *possibility* of healing and the *certainty* of the resurrection. Even those who have been healed will face death. But death can be faced in faith and in confidence of the resurrection. W. F. Bryant, an early leader in the Church of God, wrote an article about the funeral of W. B. Jones that exemplifies the Pentecostal hope.

> Before leaving their home in Cleveland a precious service was conducted by Rev. Tomlinson, in which the Holy Spirit graciously led and blessed. The remains were taken to his old home for burial . . . On our arrival . . . his sister, Josephine, stood near her brother's corpse, she felt the Spirit of praise come upon her. In yielding to it she began to glorify God and in a very few moments was speaking in other tongues as the Spirit gave utterance, which was evidence that the Comforter had come. She had never spoken in tongues before. The Spirit continued to speak through her for some time. The spirit of the message was caressing and comforting . . . The funeral service . . . was attended with the power of God, and the spirit of praises was manifested. It did not seem like a funeral, but more like a revival. They did not weep as those having no hope, but they shouted believing that they would meet their brother and son on the golden streets of the New Jerusalem (COGE, 1 Mar 1908).

The task before the Pentecostal pastor is to minister the anointed touch to the sick and dying. The anointed touch can be a powerful practice in the pastoral care of the sick and terminally ill. The wise pastor will always offer comfort and hope. Yes, there is hope in healing, and some will be healed. However, the goal of salvation is the resurrection. The presence of the elders is a demonstration of the church's care for those who suffer. The prayers and anointed touch of the elders is sacramental — a means of grace — to the suffering. All who are suffering, sick, or dying need the presence of the praying church. The praying church brings to the suffering and dying the presence of the risen Lord.

4

WATER BAPTISM

BATH OF GRACE

> Go therefore and make disciples of all the nations,
> baptizing them in the name of the Father and the Son and
> the Holy Spirit, teaching them to observe all that I
> commanded you; and lo, I am with you always, even to the
> end of the age (Matthew 28:19-20).

Once, when our youngest son, Nathan, was about eight years old
he started to enter our home after playing very hard all day. He was
filthy. He was covered in dirt and sweat. His clothes were almost
beyond salvaging, and he smelled bad. I met him at the door and
told him to remove his clothes before he entered. Then, I said to
him, "Go straight to the bathroom and get a good bath." With a
look of protest on his face, he exclaimed, "A bath! Why do I need a
bath?" He was perfectly content to live in his filth. About twenty
minutes later, he walked out of the bathroom clean and smelling
sweet. Now his presence was acceptable to live in our home once
again.

Like a young child, we tend to be content with our own filthiness.
We protest when it is suggested that we might need to clean up our
lives. Jesus told the disciples, "I go to prepare a place for you"
(John 14:2). If we desire to enter into our Father's house, we must
be presentable; we must be clean. So that we may be cleansed, God
has provided the sanctifying agents of the blood of Christ, the Holy
Spirit, and the Word of God. He has also provided water baptism.
Water baptism is a *visible* sign of *invisible* grace. But it is more.
Water baptism is a bath of grace in which the believer is spiritually

cleansed in waters upon which the Holy Spirit, the Spirit of grace, is resting. Too often we have separated the experience of salvation from water baptism, because the decision to repent and the opportunity to be baptized are normally two events separated by time. But if salvation is a series of crisis experiences along *the way of salvation*, instead of a single event, then water baptism becomes a significant encounter of grace. In this case, water baptism is a *visible* sign of *visible* grace, for the Spirit of grace should be evident in the new life of the believer, a life in which the "desire of the flesh" gives way to the "fruit of the Spirit" (Gal. 5:16-23). To put this in Pentecostal perspective, just as tongues-speech is a visible (and audible) sign of the baptism in the Holy Spirit, so water baptism is a visible sign (initial evidence) of new birth in Christ.

THE CROSS

Christian baptism has its precedent in the baptism of Jesus by John the Baptist in the Jordan River. John's baptism was a baptism of repentance, which anticipated the Messiah's baptism of Spirit and fire. John did not baptize at the Temple complex in Jerusalem, but in the wilderness of the Jordan River. John's call was for Israel to return to the waters of the Jordan through which their ancestors walked as they entered the Promised Land. Jordan baptism symbolized death to the past and birth to the future. John invited the penitent to be baptized in water as a demonstration of spiritual cleansing that is imperative for participation in God's coming kingdom.

Jesus heard John's prophetic call and responded to his invitation for "water baptism." Even though it raises some interpretive difficulties, the baptism of Jesus was a major event in the early church tradition. The apostolic witness of the New Testament is that Jesus was without sin. If the purpose of Jesus' baptism was not for cleansing from sin, why was Jesus baptized? The answer is in John's pronouncement: "Behold, the Lamb of God who takes away the sin of the world!" (John 1:29). Many Jewish converts repented and were baptized by John in the Jordan, receiving cleansing from sin. As Jesus entered the Jordan River, the sinless One was baptized in the very waters contaminated by the sins of Israel. Jesus entered the baptismal waters of Jordan as High Priest to take on Himself the sins of humanity. By submitting to John's baptism of repentance, Jesus made a vicarious confession of sin for all humanity. Paul wrote, "He made Him who knew no sin to be sin on our behalf, so that we might become the righteousness of God in Him" (2 Cor. 5:21).

Water baptism anticipates the cross. Immediately after He was baptized He entered into the wilderness temptation. Jesus spoke of His redemptive mission in terms of a baptism of suffering: "But I have a baptism to undergo, and how distressed I am until it is accomplished!" (Luke 12:50). Jesus' baptism in the Jordan was the beginning of His passion. With the Father's pronouncement, "This is My beloved Son, in whom I am well pleased," the journey to Calvary began (Matt. 3:17).

The association with the cross and water baptism was not lost on the early Christians. Martyrdom for the sake of the gospel occurred often. Stephen and James were martyred by those who sought to destroy the church (Acts 7:54-60; 12:1-2). The earliest traditions tell us that both Peter and Paul were executed in Rome. The martyrdom of the early Christians was not a tactic of guerilla warfare, but an embracing of the sufferings of Christ the Lord. Paul desired to know Christ in "the fellowship of His sufferings" (Philip. 3:10). This was not lost on early Pentecostal missionaries. In 1920, Mattie Ledbetter, an Assemblies of God missionary to China, wrote the following report:

> The Chinese were all so glad to see us home from the coast and the meetings seem very precious. God pours on the Spirit upon us often in prayer services. Several more profess salvation and are asking for baptism. Water baptism in China certainly means martyrdom, the persecutions are so great (PE, 13 Nov 1920).

REPENT AND BE BAPTIZED

Repentance is not simply the confession of sin; it must also include presenting oneself for baptism. On the Day of Pentecost, about three thousand people responded to Peter's sermon and were promptly baptized (Acts 2:41). At Samaria, Philip baptized "men and women" as they responded to the gospel (Acts 8:12). Later, Philip baptized the Ethiopian eunuch after he confessed, "I believe that Jesus Christ is the Son of God" (Acts 8:26-39). After seeing the risen Christ on the road to Damascus, Saul of Tarsus was baptized, probably by Ananias (Acts 9:10-18). The Gentile converts at Caesarea were baptized at Peter's command (Acts 10:24-48). Lydia and her household were baptized by Paul at Philippi (Acts 16:11-15). Also, the prison guard at Philippi, and his family, was baptized by Paul and Silas after hearing the gospel (Acts 16:25-34). At Corinth, Crispus, the ruler of the synagogue, and many other Corinthians received the Lord and were baptized by Paul (Acts 18:8). At Ephesus, twelve new believers were baptized after hearing the gospel of Jesus Christ (Acts 19:1-5). The example of the church in Acts tells us that the early Christians baptized all new converts. The possibility of repentance without baptism is not considered in the apostolic church. This suggests that the first Christians believed water baptism to be a significant event in *the way of salvation.*

Because the Acts of the Apostles is a primary source for Pentecostal theology, Pentecostals should be careful to follow the example of the apostolic church in the practice of water baptism. The proper understanding of baptism was one of the issues discussed at the seventh annual General Assembly of the Church of God.

> **Question.** Is water baptism obligatory when one is freed from all evil habits and sanctified?
>
> **Answer.** Yes, *all should be baptized* (italics mine), even if they have been baptized with the Holy Ghost before they were baptized with water. Acts 10:47, 48.

Question. Can the Church of God fellowship one who has not taken on the Lord in baptism?

Answer. Water baptism is not a door into the church, and is an act of obedience after one has been converted, hence the fellowship is unbroken, provided such a one will be baptized at the first opportunity, and not reject the ordinance (BM).

Pentecostals are committed to the Bible as the rule of faith. In the Bible, the baptism in the Holy Spirit is not a substitute for water baptism. Early Pentecostals were not anti-sacramental. They believed that water baptism is "obligatory" and that all converts should be "baptized at the first opportunity." Tomlinson wrote that a believer could be baptized any time after conversion, but the scriptural evidence suggested that there was to be "no delay about water baptism after conversion." Water baptism is "an essential ordinance of righteousness" (BD). The *Book of Doctrines,* a book of church order published under the auspices of the General Assembly, suggested that those who did not receive water baptism were disobedient to God's Word and would find themselves "in a backslidden condition." W. J. Seymour's *The Apostolic Faith* stated that "baptism is not a saving ordinance, but is essential because it is a command of our Lord" (AF, Sep 1907). Donald Gee, a prominent Assemblies of God leader, did not view water baptism as necessary for salvation. But he warned that refusal to be baptized was a serious offense "because such an attitude of willful neglect and rebellion reveals a condition of the heart toward God that may make us doubt the possession of that grace, which, through repentance and faith, can alone bring us salvation." Even as Gee denied the redemptive effect of water baptism, he affirmed a relationship between water baptism and saving grace. Also, he admitted that in the primitive church "an unbaptized Christian was unknown and unthought of, and for that reason it was possible to use 'baptized' and being 'in Christ' as synonymous terms" (PE, 22 Mar 1953). E. N. Bell insisted, "It never was designed that anyone should profess to have repented and not be baptized" (WE, 9 Mar 1918).

Water baptism was more than "mere form" for early Pentecostals. A. J. Tomlinson spoke of water baptism as a deeply moving, even ecstatic experience:

> Oh, if you could realize the sweet thoughts of deeper consecration and devotion as you go down into the water, perhaps with a little burden, and prayer. And the faithful minister taking you by the hand leads you down where there is water deep enough, and lifts his hands toward heaven and says: "In obedience to the command of our Lord and Savior Jesus Christ, I baptize you, my brother, in the Name of the Father, and of the Son, and of the Holy Ghost. Amen!"

> And down, down you go, buried with Christ in baptism, but as surely you rise again, the light falls full upon your face. The feeling of consecration is complete, and instead of the hesitant, just a little burdened and downcast step, all the world seems clothed in the brightness of the sun, the faces of the Christians shine as the firmament, sparkling with the fire of God's Love, for they realize just how you feel—and all seems happiness, you are light as a feather—you have been buried with Christ in baptism in the symbol, and you have risen in newness of life. And about all you can say, is "Glory to God in the highest" (BD).

If water baptism is an effectual means of grace, we must hear once again the words of Peter: "Repent, and . . . be baptized in the name of Jesus" (Acts 2:38). Genuine repentance will be expressed in water baptism, if we follow the biblical model. Both repentance and water baptism must be acts of faith, for faith in Christ is the effectual cause of regeneration. This is affirmed in the writings of the apostle Peter:

> For Christ also died for sins once for all, the just for the unjust, so that He might bring us to God, having been put to death in the flesh, but made alive in the spirit; in which also He went and made proclamation to the spirits now in prison, who once were disobedient, when the patience of God kept waiting in the days of Noah, during the construction of the ark, in which a few, that is, eight

persons, were brought safely through the water. Corresponding to that, *baptism now saves you*—not the removal of dirt from the flesh, but an appeal to God for a good conscience—through the resurrection of Jesus Christ (1 Peter 3:18-21).

Peter insisted that water baptism is, in some manner, redemptive. Water baptism is a physical and visible means of grace. Just as the ark was a physical and visible means of grace for the redemption of humanity from the flood, so water baptism is a means of grace for those who have placed their faith in the death and resurrection of Jesus Christ.

IN CHRIST

Water baptism is participation "in Christ." Water baptism signifies the believer's participation in the redemptive work of Christ. To be saved is to be "in Christ," and the church is the "body of Christ" (Rom. 12:5; 1 Cor.12:27; Eph. 4:12). Water baptism is an important motif for understanding Christ's redemptive work. Paul's audience was familiar with the rite of baptism since most of his hearers had been baptized. Therefore, the analogy between water baptism and being "in Christ" was significant in the early Christian community. In the baptism of John the Baptist, Christ took upon Himself the sins of humanity. Likewise, in water baptism the redeemed participate in Christ's death, burial, and resurrection.

In water baptism, the believer dies (Rom. 6:3). Sharing in the death of Christ is essential to Christian life. Jesus' baptism by John the Baptist anticipated the cross. When believers are baptized "in Christ," they share His cross. Paul proclaimed, "I have been crucified with Christ" (Gal. 2:20). He also wrote that "our old self was crucified with *Him*, in order that our body of sin might be done away with, so that we would no longer be slaves to sin" (Rom. 6:6). Death in Christ breaks the power of sin in our mortal bodies. Because the power of sin is broken, death is no longer master over humanity.

In water baptism, the believer is buried with Christ (Rom. 6:4). When the lifeless body of the crucified Lord rested in the tomb, the earliest Christian traditions tell us that Jesus descended into Hades. This tradition is supported in the words of 1 Peter: ". . . by whom also He went and preached to the spirits in prison" (1 Peter 3:19 NKJV). Hades is the abode of the dead. The descent into Hades establishes that Jesus Christ suffered the totality of human death. Even in death, Jesus "had to be made like His brethren in all things, so that He might become a merciful and faithful High Priest" (Heb. 2:17). In Hades, Jesus anticipated His resurrection and took possession of the keys of Hades and Death (Rev. 1:18). The power of death cannot be victorious. Water baptism is a real burial that signifies the death of a life corrupted by sin and anticipates resurrection to new life. Burial signifies the reality of death; the old life has passed. In burial, we can take nothing of this present age. The body of corruption fades into dust. Burial is a transition from this present age to the age to come (Rom. 8:18).

In water baptism, the believer shares in the resurrection of Christ, being raised to walk "in newness of life" (Rom. 6:4). Death and burial anticipate resurrection. Remember Paul's proclamation: "I have been crucified with Christ; it is no longer I who live, *but Christ lives in me*" (Gal. 2:20). Baptism means that believers are in union with Christ. The Holy Spirit and the power of the resurrected Christ are present within all believers. Therefore, believers can anticipate their own resurrection. Paul wrote, "But if the Spirit of Him who raised Jesus from the dead dwells in you, He who raised Christ from the dead will also give life to your mortal bodies through His Spirit who dwells in you" (Rom. 8:11). This is the ultimate hope of Christian faith. Christians can joyfully respond to Christ's call to "Come and die" because of the certain hope of eternal life. Water baptism anticipates the "glory that is to be revealed" (Rom. 8:11).

WATER AND SPIRIT

Nicodemas approached Jesus and inquired about the kingdom of God. In the course of the conversation, Jesus said, "Truly, truly, I say to you, unless one is born of water and the Spirit he cannot enter into the kingdom of God" (John 3:5). In answering Nicodemas, Jesus spoke of new birth by using terms that are associated with the theme of the new covenant in the prophets— water and Spirit (Ezekiel 36:24-27). Jesus told Nicodemas, salvation is from above; it is the work of God and is beyond human achievement. It is almost certain that Jesus had these words from Ezekiel in mind as He spoke with Nicodemas. Throughout Scripture, the Spirit and water are closely associated. In creation the Spirit of God hovered over the waters (Genesis 1:2). During the great Flood, Noah and his family rested safely upon the flood waters in the ark. In 1 Peter, this is interpreted as corresponding to the saving waters of baptism (1 Peter 3:20-21). As the Israelite slaves were delivered from Egypt, they passed through the waters of the Red Sea and were baptized into Moses (Exodus 14:22, 29; 15:8; Job 4:9; Psalm 78:13; 1 Cor. 10:1-2). The wilderness generation passed through the waters of the Jordan River to enter the Promised Land (Joshua 3:1ff). Jeremiah refers to the Lord as "the fountain of living waters" (Jeremiah 17:13) Jesus told the Samaritan woman, ". . . whoever drinks of the water that I will give him shall never thirst; but the water that I will give him will become in him a well of water springing up to eternal life" (John 4:14). When Jesus said that one must be born of the Spirit and water he was using a well-established tradition that associated the Spirit of God with the life-giving properties of water. So then, is water merely a metaphor for the Spirit? Or, is water, touched by the Spirit, an agent of the Spirit in creation and redemption? When Jesus told Nicodemas that new birth comes by water and the Spirit, did He mean to suggest the waters of baptism? The best way to answer these questions is to see how the early Christians interpreted the words of Jesus in the life of the church.

There can be little doubt that the church of Acts associated water baptism with initial repentance and belief in the Lord Jesus Christ. Peter proclaimed, "Repent, and each of you be baptized in the name of Jesus Christ for the forgiveness of your sins; and you will receive the gift of the Holy Spirit" (Acts 2:38). Throughout Acts, all saving acts—preaching, healing, exorcising, and baptizing—are done "in the name of Jesus Christ" because the crucified Jesus has been exalted as "Lord and Christ" by God the Father (Acts 2:26-28). Peter insists that ". . . there is no other name under heaven given among men by which we must be saved" (Acts 4:12 NKJV). The "name" represents the authority of the person. To be baptized "in the name of Jesus" affirms His authority over all earthly and spiritual powers. It is also an expression of the believer's submission and allegiance to the lordship of Christ.

WASHED BY THE SPIRIT

Water baptism is a spiritual bath. Ananias encouraged Saul of Tarsus to be quickly baptized so that his sins could be *washed away* (Acts 22:16). Paul warned the Corinthians that the unrighteous—the sexually immoral, idol worshipers, thieves and liars—will not inherit the kingdom of God. Then Paul proclaimed, "Such were some of you; but you were washed, but you were sanctified, but you were justified in the name of the Lord Jesus Christ and in the Spirit of our God" (1 Cor. 6:9-11). He wrote to Titus that Christians are saved "by the washing of regeneration and renewing by the Holy Spirit" (Titus 3:5). Later he wrote to the Ephesians that Christ would sanctify and cleanse His church "by the washing of water with the word" (Eph. 5:26). The writer of Hebrews encourages us to "draw near with a sincere heart in full assurance of faith, having our hearts sprinkled clean from an evil conscience and *our bodies washed with pure water*" (Heb. 10:22). Some New Testament scholars suggest that these texts refer not to water baptism, but to a spiritual cleansing which is affected by the Holy Spirit. This ignores the fact that the Holy Spirit is the effective agent in water baptism. Water and the Spirit are closely associated in human salvation throughout the Scriptures. To make a distinction between the saving activity of the Holy Spirit and water baptism is alien to the thought of the apostles. Nothing in the New Testament suggests that water baptism alone is sufficient for human salvation. There must be repentance and a confession of faith before one is baptized. The "washing of regeneration" is wholly the work of the Holy Spirit.

Some early Pentecostals cautiously affirmed the efficacy of water baptism. E. N. Bell wrote that water baptism "certainly does, in some sort of a sense, wash away our sins." He declared that those who denied the need for water baptism were false teachers. Bell then explained the "sense" in which baptism washes away sins: "So then, our sins are actually taken away through the blood of Christ by the power of the Holy Ghost, and they are figuratively washed away in water baptism." For Bell "figuratively" meant "likeness." In baptism, believers share in the likeness of Christ's death, and also in the likeness of Christ's resurrection (Rom. 6:5). Bell denied that the believer shares "in the real and actual death of Jesus Christ" but affirms that the believer rises from the baptismal waters "alive unto God." Bell's explanation here is muddled. It seems that he is suggesting that in baptism believers share "figuratively" in Christ's death, but "actually" in His resurrection. Bell affirmed the primacy of the blood and Spirit in the remission of sin. He does not support the doctrine of baptismal regeneration, but he sought to affirm the efficacy of water baptism, *in some sense*, in the washing away of sins. For Bell, the sacramental forms of the church represented "the pictures of realities, the symbols of glorious truth" (WE, 27 Mar 1915).

Water baptism is a sacrament, a means of saving grace, because it is so closely associated with the work of the Holy Spirit and the death and resurrection of Christ. It is a spiritual bath which looks to the resurrection of the body. We must keep in mind the nature of human salvation. We tend to think in terms of the "salvation of the soul." But the Christian view of human redemption is not limited to the spirit and/or soul. The whole human person — body, soul, and spirit—is redeemed and anticipates resurrection. Yes, the Holy Spirit is the effective agent in the washing of the person. Likewise, the Spirit resting upon the baptismal waters is the effective cause in water baptism. Water has its origin in the creative work of the Spirit. We can affirm the concept of "both/and," that is water and the Spirit. In presenting our bodies for water baptism, we present our whole self—body, soul, and spirit. Salvation is about a clean conscience and pure heart. It is also about our bodies being a temple of the Holy Spirit (1 Cor. 6:19).

The cleansing of the spiritual heart of a person has a sanctifying effect upon the physical body because spirit, soul, and body are three components of the human self. Spirit and water are a means of saving grace whereby human spirit and body are cleansed so that the whole human person — body, soul, and spirit — may be a temple of the Holy Spirit.

BAPTISM IN THE HOLY SPIRIT

Paul wrote that believers have been "baptized into Christ Jesus (Rom. 6:3) and have received the "Spirit of life" who dwells in us and bears witness that we are the children of God. The corresponding sign of baptism is the Spirit-inspired *utterance* "Abba! Father! (Rom. 8:2, 14-16). He declared, "For by one Spirit we were all baptized into one body . . . and we were all made to drink of one Spirit (1 Cor. 12:13). Paul associates water baptism with the gift of the Spirit, and the manifested signs of the Spirit include diverse spiritual gifts (1 Cor. 12:8-10) and the excellence of love (1 Cor. 12:13-13:13). Again, Paul declares that believers have been "baptized into Christ"; they have received the Spirit by faith, and the signs of the Spirit include miracles and sanctifying virtues (Gal. 3:2-7, 27; 5:22-23). Water baptism is more than a ritual cleansing; it is a charismatic encounter in the Spirit. Pentecostals throughout the world associate water baptism with exorcism and healing.

Water baptism anticipates the baptism in the Holy Spirit. John the Baptist spoke of the Messiah as one who would baptize "in the Holy Spirit and fire" (Matt. 3:11). When John baptized Jesus in the Jordan River, the heavens opened and the Holy Spirit descended upon Him. While most English translations describe a peaceful event, the Greek text describes something altogether different. The Gospel of Mark records the descent of Spirit upon Jesus with these words: "And at once, as he was coming up out of the water, he saw *the heavens torn apart* and the Spirit, like a dove, descending on him" (Mark 1:10 NJB). The descent of the Spirit upon Jesus threatened the stability of the present cosmological order and anticipated the coming kingdom. In fact, Mark's gospel begins and ends with the outpouring of the Holy Spirit. Mark begins his gospel with the account of Jesus' baptism and the descent of the Spirit. Mark concludes,

> He who has believed and has been baptized shall be saved; but he who has disbelieved shall be condemned. These signs will accompany those who have believed: in My name they will cast out demons, they will speak with new tongues; they will pick up serpents, and if they drink any deadly poison, it will not hurt them; they will lay hands on the sick, and they will recover" (Mark 16:16-18).

The implication is that the same Spirit, who is poured out upon Jesus Christ at his baptism in the Jordan River, is to be poured out upon the disciples of Jesus at their baptism. Because Jesus embodies all humanity, the descent of the Spirit upon Him at His baptism anticipates the Jerusalem Pentecost event, which is characterized by a "rushing mighty wind" and "tongues of fire" (Acts 2:1-4).

In his Pentecost message, the apostle Peter declared that the goal of Christ's redemptive work is "the gift of the Holy Spirit" (Acts 2:38-39). Jesus' crucifixion and resurrection anticipate Pentecost. In the preaching of the apostles, to be saved is to be born of the Spirit. It is the Holy Spirit who makes the blood of Jesus efficacious, regenerates penitent sinners, sanctifies the believer, effects adoption into the family of God, and by whom believers receive glorification (John 3:5; Rom. 8:11-19; 1 Cor. 6:11; 2 Thes. 2:13; Titus 3:5; 1 Peter 1:2). Water baptism is the Christian rite that represents the believer's regeneration by the Spirit and anticipates the fullness of the Spirit. Water baptism alone does not affect the new birth; neither does it confer the Holy Spirit. Cornelius' household received the Spirit with the evidence of speaking in tongues, prior to being baptized in water (Acts 10:44-48). While water baptism should not be minimized, reception of the Spirit is by faith. Peter *commanded* Cornelius and his household to be baptized in water *after* they had received the Spirit. God is free to bestow the Spirit as God wills. In this context, water baptism is a sacramental ritual signifying the church's affirmation of God's saving acts.

The relationship between water baptism and Spirit baptism is clearly demonstrated in Paul's mission at Ephesus.

> He said to them, "Did you receive the Holy Spirit when you believed?" And they said to him, "No, we have not even heard whether there is a Holy Spirit." And he said, "Into what then were you baptized?" And they said, "Into John's baptism." Paul said, "John baptized with the baptism of repentance, telling the people to believe in Him who was coming after him, that is, in Jesus." When they heard this, they were baptized in the name of the Lord Jesus. And when Paul had laid his hands upon them, the Holy Spirit came on them, and they began speaking with tongues and prophesying (Acts 19:2-6).

The promise of Pentecost is "Repent, and each of you be baptized in the name of Jesus Christ for the forgiveness of your sins; and you will receive the gift of the Holy Spirit" (Acts 2:38). The baptism of John the Baptist did not anticipate the gift of Spirit. Because the Ephesian believers had received the baptism of John, they had not received the gift of the Holy Spirit. But John anticipated the One who "is mightier than I . . . He will baptize you with the Holy Spirit" (Matt. 3:11). For the earliest Christians, the baptism of

Jesus in the Jordan River was the archetype for all Christian baptisms. It was expected that as the believers came up out of the baptismal waters, the Holy Spirit would descend upon them. Christian water baptism was more than a ritual washing; it was an encounter. After the Ephesian believers received water baptism "in the name of Jesus," Paul laid his hands on them and "the Holy Spirit came on them, and they began speaking with tongues." There is an undeniable correspondence between being water baptized in the name of Jesus and receiving the gift of the Holy Spirit.

The relationship between water baptism and Spirit baptism was not lost in the thought of some early Pentecostals. E. N. Bell wrote, "Baptism looks back to a death to sin, to a life in Christ and *forward to a baptism with the Holy Spirit*" (WE, 9 Mar 1918). Speaking in reference to the baptism of Jesus, Stanley H. Frodsham wrote:

> The Holy Spirit came down like a dove on Jesus immediately (after) He was baptized, and we should look for everyone to receive the like gift immediately (as) they come out of the water. Chrysostom in the 4th century wrote "Whoever was baptized, in apostolic days straightway spake with tongues." This was the initial physical evidence that they had received the baptism of the Holy Ghost (CE, 28 Jun 1919).

The Apostolic Faith reported on baptismal services in which the baptismal candidates were Spirit-baptized.

> On Thanksgiving Day a baptismal service was held at the Pentecostal Mission on Maple and Eighth Streets, where there is a baptistry. Twenty-four were baptized by immersion. The Spirit of God was upon the people. The candidates for baptism were filled with the Spirit and shouted and praised God as they came out of the water (AF, Dec 1906).

Baptismal services took place on the banks of the River Assimboine at this place 23 persons receiving baptism by immersion. It was a sacred occasion. The Holy Ghost witnessed through the speaking in tongues of those who were baptized (AF, Jun-Sep 1907).

Likewise, *The Christian Evangel* reported on a baptismal service in Ramsey, Illinois:

The last Sunday of the meetings three followed the Lord in the ordinance of baptism according to Matt. 28:19. The Lord put his seal of approval on the service by pouring out His Spirit on the candidates and they could hardly get out of the water, the power of God was on them in such a wonderful way (CE, 12 Jul 1919).

One believer (probably Homer Tomlinson) testified that his own experience of water baptism was a powerful and moving Pentecostal event.

In the year 1908 when I myself was baptized 128 went down into the water the same day. Without a single exception they came up beaming with the light of God upon their faces — and a shout in their hearts, and many broke out in praises, even speaking in other tongues as on the day of Pentecost, about which we have studied previously. There is nothing like obedience to make your soul feel the Pentecostal blessing. In fact, there have been many instances of which I myself have heard when those who followed the Lord obediently in water baptism, were baptized with the Holy Ghost and began to speak in other tongues as they came up out of the water — just as Jesus received the Holy Ghost immediately after He was baptized in Jordan (BD).

Pentecostal baptismal services were dynamic events in which "the power of God was wonderfully manifested in divers ways; some falling into trances, some dancing in the Spirit, some singing in the Spirit, with many other manifestations of power" (CE, 5 Oct 1918). Many first-generation Pentecostals experienced Spirit baptism as they were baptized in water. And, it seems that they expected this to be normative for all believers. E. N. Bell wrote, "As soon as one truly repents and accepts Christ as Savior, he should at once be baptized in water and look for God to pour out His Spirit upon him." He believed that many who were seeking Spirit-baptism were "struggling and hanging around the altar for months" without receiving the promise because of their disobedience in ignoring water baptism. He declared, "We have neither apostolic precept nor example for praying our heads off to get people baptized with the Holy Ghost before they are baptized in water." He viewed the outpouring of the Spirit upon the house of Cornelius prior to water baptism as an aberration and insisted that "the apostolic custom points also to the praying for the Spirit upon believers ONLY AFTER they have been baptized" (CE, 16 Nov 1918).

A second generation Church of God leader, D. C. Boatwright, wrote that water baptism after repentance is essential if one's salvation is to be "enjoyed in the fullest measure." Although Boatwright rejected that water baptism imparted *saving* grace, he insisted that baptism was essential to "fulfill all righteousness," that is, to be obedient to the command of Christ. It could be inferred that Boatwright, with his contemporaries, understood water baptism as *sanctifying* grace. If the new convert was to enjoy salvation in its fullest measure — sanctification and Spirit baptism — then the new convert must walk in obedience to the Scriptures and be baptized in water. Full obedience to God's Word is where "the Christian's power lies." Further, Boatwright suggested a correspondence between water baptism and Spirit baptism. He said, "I honestly believe that one reason so many find it difficult to receive the baptism with the Holy Ghost is because they have not taken this profound truth seriously enough." In his view, submission to water baptism as an act of obedience was, in some manner, preparatory for Spirit baptism (COGE, 22 Oct 1949).

The baptismal waters have a sanctifying effect in preparing the believer for the reception of the Holy Spirit, "who is about to come upon us." This is what happened when Paul preached at Ephesus—

new believers were baptized in the Spirit shortly after being baptized in water (Acts 19:5). The words of Jesus in Mark's Gospel suggest that signs – exorcisms, tongues, and healings – are associated with water baptism (Mark 16:16-18).

Water baptism anticipates baptism in the Holy Spirit in *way of salvation*. Pentecostals have long affirmed that signs follow baptized believers, specifically tongues-speech. Water baptism and Spirit baptism are related redemptive experiences in *the way of salvation*, but they are distinct. As we have seen, Spirit baptism may precede water baptism as an event in time. A believer may be baptized in the Spirit upon rising out of the baptismal waters. But just as regeneration and Spirit baptism are distinct experiences in *the way of salvation*, so is water baptism and Spirit baptism. Water baptism anticipates Spirit baptism; and it may serve an as analogy for Spirit baptism. But water baptism is not Spirit baptism.

A DOOR

Many Pentecostals do not view water baptism as a "door into the church." This represents a disjointed view. As we have discussed earlier, if life in the church is to be meaningful in the Pentecostal *way of salvation,* then Pentecostals must insist on the necessity of repentance, new birth, water baptism, and life in the church. Early adherents of the Church of God believed water baptism and church membership to be essential in the "divine order" of salvation. J. L. Thornhill wrote, "The expression born into the kingdom; baptized into the body; then joined or added to the church is divine order . . . It was an apostolic practice in the early church" (COGE, 28 Apr 1923). The church teaches, nourishes, supports, and graciously disciplines believers so that believers may be properly discipled. Membership in the church must is the ongoing sanctification of the believer in *the way of salvation.*

In Acts, we find that repentance, water baptism, and life in the church are significant and interrelated events in *the way of salvation.* "So then, those who had received his word were baptized; and that day there were added about three thousand souls" (Acts 2:41). The church is the fellowship of the baptized. Baptism is the sacramental sign through which believers enter. Water baptism incorporates the believer into the body of Christ which is the church — a single body with many members (1 Cor. 12:14, 20, 27). Christ himself is the head of the body (Eph. 4:15; 5:23). To be outside of the church is to be outside of the body of Christ. Paul wrote, "For by one Spirit we were all baptized into one body — whether Jews or Greeks, whether slaves or free — and we were all made to drink of one Spirit" (1 Cor. 12:13). One might object that Paul here is speaking of Spirit baptism, not water baptism. But we have already observed that throughout the New Testament, the Holy Spirit is the effective agent in water baptism and that water baptism anticipates Spirit baptism. In this context, Paul is referring to Spirit-infused water baptism. Further, water baptism is participation "in Christ," and the church is the "body of Christ." Water baptism and Spirit baptism are related experiences in *the way of salvation*. The pledge of water baptism is fulfilled in Spirit baptism.

The church is a community in covenant with God bound together by a common confession and encounter that Jesus Christ is Lord. The earliest creedal statements of the Christian church were baptismal confessions. The earliest baptismal confession is recorded by Luke:

> Now as they went down the road, they came to some water. And the eunuch said, "See, here is water. What hinders me from being baptized?" Then Philip said, "If you believe with all your heart, you may." And he answered and said, *"I believe that Jesus Christ is the Son of God"* (Acts 8:36-37 NKJV).

The confession "Jesus is Lord" is inspired by the Holy Spirit. When Peter confessed, "You are the Christ," Jesus responded, "Blessed are you, Simon Barjona, because flesh and blood did not reveal this to you, but My Father who is in heaven" (Matt. 16:17). Paul wrote, ". . . no one can say that 'Jesus is Lord' except by the Holy Spirit" (1

Cor. 12:3). This confession is the life-seed of the church. From this confession all spiritual life springs forth.

The church is a visible communion. Pentecostals have tended to understand water baptism and Spirit baptism in terms of an individual encounter, with little attention being given to the corporate dimension. Again, the baptism of Jesus is the archetype. Jesus, as the incarnate Word, represents the whole of humanity. The descent of the Spirit upon Jesus signifies the Spirit being poured out upon all flesh as seal and pledge which anticipates the fullness of God. To be baptized in water and sealed by the Spirit is to be incorporated into the body of Christ (Rom. 6:3; 1 Cor. 12:13; Gal. 3:27; Eph. 4:4-5). Being baptized into the body of Christ—the church—is more than a "mystical" or "spiritual" reality. Water baptism is a visible event that signifies being incorporated into the visible church. The church is to be a witness to the world. The church is how the world *sees* Christ. Jesus said, "By this all men will know that you are My disciples, if you have love for one another" (John 13:35). Christian love is demonstrated by visible acts of mercy to the hungry, poor, strangers, and prisoners (Matt. 25:31-46). The church is a divine-human institution, a living body that exists as a visible reality in this world. The unity of the Faith is the Spirit-inspired baptismal confession that "Jesus is Lord." Because all Christians are united in Christ and Spirit, the unity of the church is the prayer of Christ and the work of the Spirit.

The church is a visible community that exists as a single corporate entity with a diversity of members. The church is comprised of male and female, Gentile and Jew, and rich and poor. In this diverse community there is to be no distinction (Acts 15:6-9; Rom. 10:12; Gal. 3:28; Jas. 2:1-4). This is a testimony to the unity of humanity in Christ. However, we must admit that the church has not always demonstrated this unity. If we carefully examine ourselves, we will find that too often we have been a divided community. Paul warned against the church's tendency to be schismatic. The Corinthian believers were divided by their allegiance to charismatic church leaders and by economic class (1

Cor. 1:10-15; 10:18-22). Paul insisted that these divisions do not reflect the essential unity of the church as the one body of Christ.

The church is a community in which all humans are made equal. Baptism is the bath of new creation in which the Holy Spirit washes away the stain of sin, renews the believer, signifies adoption into the family of God and unites the believer with Christ (Acts 22:16; Rom. 6:5; 1 Cor. 6:11; Gal. 3:26; Eph. 5:26; Titus 3:5). Because baptism is to be united with Christ, in baptism the dividing wall and enmity that has separated humans is washed away. Therefore, baptism should be a sign that points the way toward a more Christian personal and social ethic. In this old age – the age of the flesh – Gentiles, slaves, and women are of an inferior status. Jews, freemen, and males are assumed to have priority. However, in the new creation – the age of the Spirit signified by water baptism – Gentiles, slaves, and women inherit a new status.

The apostolic church understood the significance of baptism for men *and women*. When many Samaritans responded in faith to the preaching of Philip, Luke records that "they were being baptized, men *and women alike*" (Acts 8:12). This demonstrates that baptism for men *and women* was the standard Christian initiation in the apostolic church. This is a significant event when we remember that the covenant sign of Abraham was circumcision. The rite of circumcision could only be performed upon males, therefore women were restricted. The correspondence between the Jewish ritual of circumcision and Christian water baptism was significant in the mind of Paul.

> . . . and in Him you were also circumcised with a circumcision made without hands, in the removal of the body of the flesh by the circumcision of Christ; having been buried with Him in baptism, in which you were also raised up with Him through faith in the working of God, who raised Him from the dead (Col. 2:11-12).

"The circumcision of Christ" is a metaphorical reference to his violent death on the cross. The phrase "a circumcision made without hands" refers to the work of the Holy Spirit in the transformation of humanity. Christian baptism is to share in the death and resurrection of Christ, and is associated with reception of the Holy Spirit. Many of the errors and heresies that proliferated in the apostolic church concerned circumcision. In fact, the circumcision of Gentile believers was the primary issue discussed at the Jerusalem conference (Acts 15). If the leaders of the apostolic church had affirmed the necessity of circumcision, then women would have been restricted from full participation in the church. Long after the matter was settled at Jerusalem the issue continued to trouble the early church. Regarding the issue of circumcision, Paul was adamant that water baptism is the all-sufficient sign of being "in Christ." Therefore, women are full participants in Christ and in Christ's church.

Likewise slavery, a human institution of this corrupted present age, is washed away by the waters of baptism. Paul offers a glimpse of how slavery is to pass away. In his letter to Philemon, Paul refers to Onesimus, the runaway slave as "my child" (Philemon 10) and he encourages Philemon to receive Onesimus as "a beloved brother" (Philemon 16). This request is made possible only because in Christ the old order is passing away, the new is coming. Being "in Christ" transforms relationships and forms a new human fellowship in which all believers are sons and daughters, brothers and sisters, mothers and fathers. No longer could Onesimus be considered enslaved property; rather "in Christ" his full humanity is restored. Also, in writing to Timothy, Paul declared,

> But we know that the Law is good, if one uses it lawfully, realizing the fact that law is not made for a righteous person, but for those who are lawless and rebellious, for the ungodly and sinners, for the unholy and profane, for those who kill their fathers or mothers, for murderers and immoral men and homosexuals and *kidnappers* and liars and perjurers, and whatever else is *contrary to sound teaching*, according to the glorious gospel of the blessed God, with which I have been entrusted (1 Tim. 1:8-11).

The word *kidnappers* is translated as *menstealers* (KJV) or *slave traders* (as in ESV, NLT, NRSV). Paul views slavery as "contrary to sound teaching." The oppression or enslavement of any human being is an offense to the gospel of Jesus Christ (Rom. 8:21; 2 Cor. 3:17; Gal. 5:1). In the new creation all social and political distinctions of the old order are passing away. As we continue to struggle with issues of oppression, race, and immigration throughout the world Christians must approach these issues from the perspective of being baptized in Christ. In the new creation all humans – Jews and Gentiles, free and slave, male and female – share in the glory of Christ.

Water baptism affirms the universal priesthood of all believers. Water baptism is the primary sacrament of the church. All believers come to Christ in the same manner: by a call from the Holy Spirit and through the waters of baptism. As the primary sacrament, all members of the church enter through the same door. Water baptism is the common experience and confession of all believers. Because water baptism corresponds with church membership in the *way of salvation*, pastors and church leaders should insist that those who present themselves for baptism likewise join the church; and those who seek church membership should be baptized. Christian practice should be a reflection of Christian theology. In commissioning His apostles, Jesus established baptism as the initiation rite for those answering His call to salvation and discipleship (Matt. 28:19-20). Jesus said, "He who has believed and has been baptized shall be saved; but he who has disbelieved shall be condemned" (Mark 16:16). Believing and baptism are faith responses to the call of salvation.

Believing and baptism are the initial experiences of grace. The *way of salvation* also includes being a disciple. To be a disciple is to be instructed in the faith. In commissioning His apostles, Jesus said:

> Go therefore and *make disciples* of all the nations, *baptizing them* in the name of the Father and the Son and the Holy Spirit, *teaching them* to observe all that I commanded you; and lo, I am with you always, even to the end of the age (Matt. 28:19-20).

Disciple-making requires "baptizing them" *and* "teaching them." Developing a structured program of discipleship training will be a challenge for a Pentecostal culture which favors spontaneity and resists formal education. Pentecostals should affirm that Christian discipleship begins with an initial sanctifying *encounter* and continues in a sanctifying *process*. This sanctifying process is the nurture of the church. Believers are sanctified by the Holy Spirit, the blood of Christ, and the Word of God. To be educated in the theology and ethics of the Christian faith is a sanctifying process. The church as a Spirit-formed and Spirit-filled community is endowed with Spirit-inspired teachers for this very purpose. Spirit-inspired teachers assure the transformation and acculturation of new believers in the church. If the church fails in this ministry, there is high probability that water baptism will become a formal rite rather than a transforming encounter.

In the Name of the Father, Son, and Spirit

Early Pentecostal proclamation was focused on Christ. Jesus Christ is Savior, Sanctifier, Healer, Spirit Baptizer, and soon coming King. As is often the case in renewal movements, early enthusiasm can lead to the development of questionable, even heretical theology. During the formative years of the movement, Pentecostalism was threatened by a major theological controversy. After the Azusa Street revival, some leaders began espousing a "new issue" relating to the use of Jesus' name. Because miracles were being performed "in Jesus name," it was suggested water baptism should also be performed in the name of Jesus only. Proponents of this practice looked to scriptural examples in Acts. Repentant sinners are saved and baptized in the name of Jesus (Acts 2:38; 8:12, 16; 10:48; 16:31; 19:5). Believers received the gift of the Holy Spirit in the name of Jesus (Acts 2:38). The sick are healed in the name of Jesus (Acts 3:6, 16; 4:10, 30). Demons are exorcised in the name of Jesus (Acts 16:18). Believers were persecuted for the name of Jesus (Acts 5:40; 15:26; 21:13). Christians worshiped in the name of Jesus

(Acts 19:17). This led to a "new revelation" concerning the nature of God. According to those labeled "oneness" Pentecostals, the names "Father, Son, and Spirit" did not represent three eternally distinct persons who share one divine essence, but a threefold manifestation of one divine being.

While it appeared to be a "new issue," Oneness Pentecostal theology is a revival of a third-century heresy known as "modalism." Modalism denies that God exists eternally as Father, Son, and Spirit. Rather, through the ages, God is revealed in various temporary modes. An unfortunate effect of the "hyper-Christology" of oneness Pentecostalism is that it actually denies the essential nature of the Incarnation as the permanent union between God and humanity. Most early Pentecostals recognized the mistake of Oneness Pentecostalism and embraced the orthodox Trinitarian and Christological teachings of the ancient church as expressed in the Nicene Creed. The Trinitarian baptismal formula is preferred in order that the Father, Son, and the Holy Spirit are equally glorified in human redemption. Although apostolic ministry was done "in the name of Jesus Christ," it was not at the exclusion of the Father and the Holy Spirit. Jesus Christ is affirmed as Son and Savior by the Father and the Spirit through miracles, the greatest of which is the resurrection. The Spirit is the "promise of the Father" and is given through the Son. Salvation is consistently presented in terms of Trinitarian redemptive activity.

The Trinitarian baptismal formula affirms the deity of Jesus Christ. In early Jewish Christianity, the deity of the Father and the Spirit was assumed, even if the personal distinctions between them were not. The inclusion of "and of the Son" in the early baptismal creed was an effort to insist upon the deity of Jesus and His equality with God the Father. The early theologians affirmed the dogma of the Holy Trinity in order to protect Jewish monotheism, as well as offer an explanation as to how Jesus, the son of Mary, could also exist eternally as God the Son. Oneness Pentecostalism denies the eternal sonship of Christ, which also ultimately denies His personal distinction as God the Son.

The Trinitarian baptismal formula affirms the deity and personal distinction of the Holy Spirit. In "oneness" Pentecostalism, the personal distinction and deity of the Holy Spirit is diminished. The equality of the Spirit with the Father and the Son is vitally important in redemption. The Spirit effected the Incarnation (Matt. 1:18, 20; Luke 1:35); anointed and empowered Jesus for His messianic ministry (Matt. 3:16; Luke 3:22; 4:1); was active in the resurrection of Jesus (Rom. 8:11); and proceeds from the Father and from (or through) the Son (John 14:26; 15:26; Acts 2:33). Through the redemptive activity of the Holy Spirit, penitent sinners receive the full blessing of salvation. The Spirit creates the redemptive community (2 Cor. 13:14). If the Holy Spirit is less than God, then Jesus, the child of Mary, is less than God, and the whole economy of redemption is without effect.

Even as the Trinitarian formula is preferred, we must concede that baptism "in the name of Jesus" is attested in the Acts of the Apostles as a biblical baptismal formula. Some early Pentecostals sought to remain faithful to the teaching of Holy Scriptures and embrace both baptismal formulas. In a response to the "Jesus only" controversy, E. N. Bell wrote that there are "scriptural varieties" of the baptismal formula and that any scriptural formula is proper as long as it is "done in good faith" and not to the exclusion of other biblical formulas (WE, 3 Jul 1915). The Church of God *Book of Doctrines* offered two baptism formulas to be used by ministers.

> In obedience to the command of our Lord and Savior Jesus Christ, I now baptize you, my brother, in the name of the Father, and of the Son, and of the Holy Ghost. Amen.

Or,

> Upon your confession of faith in the Lord Jesus Christ, I now baptize you, Brother Davis, in the name of the Father, and of the Son, and of the Holy Ghost.

Early Pentecostals sought to remedy the contention of the Oneness controversy by including the name of Jesus within the Trinitarian formula.

MODE OF BAPTISM

The word *baptize* means "to dip in or under," "to dye," "to immerse," "to sink," "to drown," "to bathe," and/or "wash." From the Biblical language, there can be little doubt that the proper mode of water baptism is immersion. Further, since water baptism is participation in the death, burial, and resurrection of Jesus Christ, the physical and visual impact of complete immersion in water suggest it to be the normative mode. But not all Pentecostals have insisted on immersion. *The Discipline of the Pentecostal Holiness Church* (1908) stated, "All candidates for baptism shall have the right of choice between the modes of baptism as practiced by the various evangelical denominations." Even as we are committed to immersion as the proper mode for water baptism, pastors should be open to other modes when immersion is not practical. For those who might object, I remind them of the thief on the cross. With no opportunity to receive baptism, Jesus promised that the thief would enter Paradise. This biblical example suggests that when necessary there is some freedom in baptismal practices.

5

THE LORD'S SUPPER

BREAD OF LIFE, CUP OF BLESSING

> And when He had taken *some* bread *and* given thanks, He broke it and gave it to them, saying, "This is My body which is given for you; do this in remembrance of Me." And in the same way *He took* the cup after they had eaten, saying, "This cup which is poured out for you is the new covenant in My blood" (Luke 22:19-20).

Once, I was leading a worship service for ministerial candidates. The worship service followed a session in which I taught on the sacraments of the church. At the conclusion of the session, I invited the participants to the altar to pray for one another. As we anointed and laid hands on the participants, the Holy Spirit began to move. I offered the bread and cup as people wept, shouted, and worshiped in tongues. It was evident to all that we were in the "real presence" of God. A few days later, a colleague who participated in that holy meal said to me, "I left that service feeling so full." Jesus said, "Blessed are those who hunger and thirst for righteousness for they shall be filled (Matt. 5:6).

The meal is a prominent theological motif throughout the Scriptures. In the midst of the Garden of Eden, God provided the Tree of Life and the Tree of the Knowledge of Good and Evil (Genesis 2:9). The fruit of the Tree of Life was a holy meal, a meal of grace, blessing, and eternal life. The fruit of the Tree of the Knowledge of Good and Evil was an unholy meal that poisoned humanity and resulted in death. During Israel's wilderness journey, God provided manna from heaven, even though the people yearned for the food of Egypt (Numbers 11:4-6). When the prophet Elijah hid by the Brook Cherith during a drought and famine, the Lord sent ravens to bring him bread and meat (1 Kings 17:1-6). The psalmist's description of the Word of God was that it tasted as sweet as honey (Psalms 19:10; 119:103. Isaiah prophesied a banquet hosted by the Lord to which all the people of the earth are invited (Isaiah 25:6-8).

The feeding miracles are prominent in the Gospels. These miracles provide theological motifs that introduce Jesus as the fulfillment of Jewish Messianic expectations. The feeding miracles of Moses occurred in a barren wilderness, whereas the feeding miracles of Jesus took place in the grassy meadows of Galilee (Matt. 14:19; Mark 6:39). The manna God provided Israel was fresh for a day and then spoiled. The feeding miracles of Jesus reflect no such tendencies; leftovers were collected to be used in feeding others or perhaps a later meal. These miracle stories not only look back on redemption's history, but they also look forward and anticipate the consummation of redemption to be fulfilled at a future heavenly banquet.

Mark presents two feeding miracles, one for Israel, the other for Gentiles, to demonstrate the universal character of Jesus' redemptive mission (Mark 6:34ff; 8:1ff). Matthew's account of the feeding miracles occurs in the context of Jesus' healing ministry (Matt. 14:14; 15:30, 31). The feeding miracles anticipate the Lord's Supper. In each story, Jesus took bread, broke bread, gave thanks and ate as an act of remembrance. Luke begins his Gospel by referring to the significance of the messianic meal and concludes with a celebration of the symbolism of the messianic meal (Luke 1:53; 24:41-43). John presents Jesus, God incarnate, as the sinless sacrificial Lamb (John 1:14, 29). John's feeding miracle occurs during Passover when the Pascal Lamb became a meal of remembrance, as well as advance celebration of the imminent death of Jesus as the last Lamb (Exodus 12:8; John 6:4). John provides further insight in the discourse where Jesus identified

Himself as the "bread of life" and "living bread which came down from heaven" (John 6:31-58).

The gospel stories of Jesus' table fellowship are significant in the understanding of the Lord's Supper. Jews, Gentiles, and sinners, "the poor and the maimed and the lame and the blind" were all welcomed (Luke 14:21). Jesus was anointed for His substitutionary death at the sacramental Table (Matt. 26:6-12; Mark 14:3-8). Jesus is present at the Table and the Table is a place where sinners find mercy and receive forgiveness (Luke 7:37-50). Jesus' disciples discovered the Table to be a place where discipleship was formed and their faith challenged. All Jesus' disciples, past and present, share the cup of Christ's redemptive sufferings at the Table (Matt. 20:22, 23; Mark 10:38, 39). It is at the Table of the Lord that the disciples are taught the true nature of discipleship—disciples are to be servants (Mark 14:29, 30). Peter and Judas both experienced judgment at the Lord's Table (Matt. 26:33-35; Luke 22:21, 31-34; John 13:18, 26-27). In Mark's account of the Last Supper, the Twelve were confronted by Jesus and exposed as lacking in their devotion to Him (Mark 14:29-30). In Luke, the Table is where the resurrected Christ revealed Himself to His disciples who were slow to comprehend the reality of the resurrection (Luke 24:13-35). In John, during a meal with the resurrected Christ, Peter finds forgiveness for his threefold denial of Christ (John 21:15-17). The Table of the Lord is a place where the fallen are received and restored by our Lord.

REMEMBERING CHRIST'S DEATH

The celebration of the Lord's Supper summons the church to remember the sacrificial death of Christ. Jesus met with His disciples on the eve of His passion to eat a meal and said,

> I have earnestly desired to eat this Passover with you
> before I suffer; for I say to you, I shall never again eat it
> until it is fulfilled in the kingdom of God. And when He had
> taken a cup and given thanks, He said, "Take this and share

it among yourselves; for I say to you, I will not drink of the fruit of the vine from now on until the kingdom of God comes." And when He had taken some bread and given thanks, He broke it and gave it to them, saying, "This is My body which is given for you; *do this in remembrance of Me.*" And in the same way He took the cup after they had eaten, saying, "This cup which is poured out for you is the new covenant in My blood" (Luke 22:15-20).

The words "do this in remembrance of Me" are as representative of the Christian faith as is the cross and they are inseparable from Christian worship. Christian worship is the sacred act of remembering, that is, re-enacting or re-living an event. The observance of the Lord's Supper is an on-going divine drama that is to be repeatedly performed so that the Christ-story will be told over and over again. Songs and sermons may faithfully tell the story; but it is only as worshipers observe the Lord's Supper that they participate in the event.

Passover is the theological motif that informs the church's understanding of the Lord's Supper. In fact, it was Jesus, the Lamb of sacrifice, who reinterpreted and fulfilled Passover through His sacrificial death. The Passover meal tutored many generations of Hebrews about their miraculous deliverance from Egyptian slavery (Exodus 12:25-27). Without the Passover, succeeding generations would have been born in bondage. Therefore, Passover was more than a historic remembrance of an event that liberated their ancestors; it was an annual reenactment celebrating the liberation of successive generations. The Passover as the "First Supper" anticipates the "Last Supper," the meal in which Jesus, as High Priest, offered Himself as the sacrificial lamb for the redemption of all humanity. When Christians gather at the Table of the Lord, it is to remember the sacrificial death of Christ and, thus, the past event becomes present. It is not simply to recall a past redemptive event; it reminds believers that they are participants in an ongoing redemptive event. To remember Christ's passion through the Lord's Supper is to *re-live* the event, to *re-enact* the drama, to participate in the story.

W. J. Seymour believed the Lord's Supper was the "Christian Passover." He wrote, "the passing over the Red Sea . . . was a type of the blood of Jesus Christ that gives us victory over all the powers of the enemy." Just as the Exodus Passover was deliverance for the children of Israel, the Lord's Supper as Passover points to "our great deliverance," that is, the coming of the Lord. Just as the Exodus Passover reminded the Israelites of God's redemptive love, the Lord's Supper is a memorial of God's redemptive love in Jesus Christ. Just as the children of Israel were nourished by the body of the lamb, the Lord's Supper is healing and health to all believers who partake by faith. Seymour proclaimed, "Our souls are built up, for we eat His flesh and drink His blood" (AF, Dec 1906).

THE LORD'S SUPPER
IN THE APOSTOLIC CHURCH

The significance of the Lord's Supper among early Christian communities has significant implications for Pentecostal worship. Paul's first letter to the church at Corinth is primary to Pentecostal theology, especially as it relates to the spiritual gifts. It is interesting how Paul moved to a discussion of the spiritual gifts immediately after concluding a discussion regarding the Lord's Supper. This suggests that liturgical rites and charismatic manifestations were significant issues in the earliest Christian churches. Paul does not object to "a *form* of godliness," but to a form of godliness in which the power of God is denied (2 Tim. 3:5). In his instructions regarding the spiritual gifts Paul wrote, "But all things must be done properly and in an orderly manner" (1 Cor. 14:40). Paul insists that liturgy and spiritual gifts be governed by a dual concern for "order *and* power" (1 Cor. 11:34; 14:40). Religious practices should manifest the Spirit's *power*, and charismatic manifestations should demonstrate the Spirit's *order*. Sometimes, Pentecostals struggle with the tension that exists between manifestations of the Holy Spirit and the maintenance of order in worship. Some Pentecostals believe that any effort at maintaining order quenches the Spirit's fire. Pentecostal pastors are charged with the responsibility to lead worship in which the Spirit is not quenched and the worshiper is free to respond to the moving of the Holy Spirit. In doing so, the pastor must be aware that sometimes a *lack of order* can quench the Holy Spirit.

The celebration of the Lord's Supper was a central feature of worship for the early church (Acts 20:7). Like other first-century Christian churches, the Corinthian church met regularly, probably weekly, to celebrate the Lord's Supper. Paul offered the following instruction about worship: "Therefore when you meet together, it is not to eat the Lord's Supper, for in your eating, each one takes his own supper first" (1 Cor. 11:20-21). In most first century churches the celebration of the Lord's Supper was preceded by the agape feast, which was a common fellowship meal. At the agape feast there was often discrimination between the rich and poor. This was an offense to the nature of Christian fellowship. Paul's instructions to the Corinthian church regarding the separation of the agape feast from the Lord's Supper may have been the beginning of separating the two for all churches. The Corinthians' practice of joining the agape feast with the Lord's Supper was an innovation that displeased Paul. Paul's objection was not their regularity in observing the Lord's Supper. He objected to the improper manner by which they observed the Lord's Supper. Again, Paul's concern is for power *and* order. Their improper worship denied the power of the holy meal to bring the people of God into a holy communion. It should be noted, however, that Paul affirms the Lord's Supper as essential and normative in early Christian worship. Paul proposes two things in this Corinthian discourse: first, to reestablish proper order in worship and, second, to return to the earlier tradition of the Lord's Supper (1 Cor. 11:23-26). For Paul, proper observance of the Lord's Supper was normative to Christian worship.

"THIS IS MY BODY"

The Lord's Supper is a simple yet profound meal whose common elements, the loaf and the cup, carry controversial theological implications in the Christian church. The statement of Jesus, "This is my body . . . this is my blood," has been the subject of much debate. Because many Pentecostals reject the primacy of the Lord's Supper in worship, there has been limited discussion among Pentecostals as to how Christ is present in the Lord's Supper.

The celebration of the Lord's Supper was a primary act of worship in the early church. For these early believers, Christ's presence in the bread and cup is firmly based on the Incarnation. Jesus Christ, the "enfleshed Word," offered Himself to be "broken and poured out" for the redemption of all people. The bread and cup of the Lord's Supper are an extension of the Incarnation. Through prayer, the Word and the Spirit bread and cup are the flesh and blood of Jesus Christ. By receiving the Lord's Supper humans are nourished to eternal life which is resurrection to immortality in a body of flesh and blood.

PARTAKERS OF DIVINE NATURE

In the celebration of the Lord's Supper, believers are partakers of the divine nature. The Holy Spirit was active in the birth, ministry, and crucifixion of Jesus. The Eternal Word was enfleshed by Spirit in the womb of the Virgin Mary (Matt. 1:18; Luke 1:35). It was through the Spirit that Jesus ministered as the anointed One of God (Luke 4:1, 14, 18). Jesus was raised from the dead by the Spirit, and by the Spirit His sacrifice for sin is eternally efficacious (Acts 2:24; Rom. 8:11; Heb. 9:14). Through Christ's priestly ministry, humanity is sanctified so we can receive the Spirit (Heb. 10:22; 1 Peter 1:2). The Holy Spirit comes through the intercession of Jesus (John 14:16-17; 15:26; 16:7; Acts 2:33). Through the Spirit, Christ comes to believers in the bread and cup.

Some early Pentecostals used a "drinking" metaphor when speaking of the essence of the Pentecostal encounter. David Wesley Myland said that being baptized in the Holy Spirit was like swallowing "God liquidized." Pentecostals have affirmed that God's energies can be transferred to material objects, or that God's anointing is tangible, that is, "touchable." Therefore, Pentecostals should have little difficulty in understanding the Lord's Supper as worship in which the believer can touch and taste the divine.

Although early Pentecostals resisted liturgical rites in worship, they embraced the Lord's Supper with great devotion. A. J. Tomlinson wrote that partaking of the Lord's Supper is one of "the most sacred and hallowed moments in the entire Christian life" (BD). Reporting on an observance of the Lord's Supper, he wrote,

> As the bread was broken and mention made of the broken body of Jesus, He seemed to manifest His presence in the midst. As I stood there in the presence of God and before the large audience with the broken bread; a piece in each hand, I seemed to get a broader view of the Christ and wonderful scheme of redemption than ever before (COGE, 15 Jul 1910).

Tomlinson's reflection suggests an encounter that is much more than a memorial. Christ is present and the "broken bread" reveals the mystery of redemption. In an early Sunday school lesson "from a Pentecostal viewpoint," the writer offers an explanation of how believers partake in the divine nature at the Lord's Table.

> As we come to the communion table, behind the symbol and the sign, we are to see our precious Savior and to appropriate and partake of Him. It is His desire to communicate Himself to us and as we partake in faith, discerning Him whilst we feed, we receive life for our spirits, souls, and bodies.

> As the showbread was placed anew, every Sabbath, on the table before the Lord . . . so the Lord's death was shown, or announced afresh at the Lord's table [sic] on the first day of every week in the primitive Church. We need to continue steadfastly in the apostles' doctrine and fellowship and in the breaking of bread (CE, 12 Jul 1919).

J. Roswell Flower, an early leader in the Assemblies of God, wrote an article on "the sacrament of the Lord's Supper" that is wonderfully sacramental. Flower wrote that the Lord's Supper is a "visible means" of promoting "the maintenance of spiritual life through personal communion with God" and that the Lord's Supper feeds the believer's "spiritual nature for a healthy growth in the Spirit." When Flower writes about the cup and the loaf of the holy meal, it is evident that he believes there is more here than mere symbol. Concerning the cup he writes:

> When the fruit of the vine was being partaken of, we have been conscious of melting, weeping, praising, and adoring among those receiving it . . . The fruit of the vine speaks to us of the spilled Blood in which we see our sins forgiven . . . We grasp it readily and our hearts are broken again and again in deep appreciation of the benefits of Calvary.

As he writes concerning the significance of the bread, his words portray a deep sacramental devotion:

> . . . [the bread] was composed of fine flour. This speaks to the perfection of the humanity of Christ . . . And the flour was mingled with oil. The oil, of course, speaks of the Holy Ghost. Here we have the mingling of the perfect human nature of the Lord Jesus with the Divine.

As to the significance of the believer's participation in this sacrament, Flower wrote:

> Just as the manna must be gathered daily to sustain life, so we too must draw nigh daily to partake of Christ; we must hold daily communion with Him if we are to be sustained by His life . . . May God grant a deepening of our life of communion with Him, for a fuller manifestation of His life in us (PE, 2 Apr 1932).

This is not to suggest that early Pentecostals held to a Catholic or Lutheran view of the Lord's Supper. They often outright rejected such views. But, it seems that early Pentecostal leaders intuitively knew that there is a "presence" inherent in the holy meal. Baptism in the Holy Spirit brought into their lives a "real presence" that anointed the sacred acts of worship. This understanding of "real presence" became associated with the Lord's Supper. It is evident that Pentecostals believed that at the Table, through the power of the Holy Spirit, Christ is present. D. W. Kerr wrote:

> There is nothing old or stale about this memorial feast, the fruit of the vine is not old, the shed blood is not aged, the bread is not stale, the Lord's body is not a mere thing of the past, the way is new and living. The thing most striking about the character of the feast is *its presentness*, not its pastness or its futureness. *It has a present aspect*, there is a sign of warmth, the blood is not cold and coagulated but flowing fresh from the wounded side of Jesus . . . *Here is the present tense of Calvary.* We have come to a place of freshness, the result of Calvary. What is it? Life and life more abundant!

The Pentecostal encounter of the Holy Spirit baptism led early leaders of the movement to revise much of the received Christian tradition. Sometimes, they lacked the theological language to clearly express what they were experiencing or thinking. This became especially evident when they wrote about the sacraments.

> Faith can grasp mysteries that are unexplainable. Faith enters into a realm far beyond the sphere of understanding, and can extract the good and joy out of what soars high above our reasonings. We have no need to preach a doctrine of consubstantiation nor of transubstantiation; we just receive Jesus' words and act on them. "Whoso eateth my flesh and drinketh my blood, hath everlasting life" (WE, 28 Oct 1916).

This is the language of mystery—a supernatural truth that defies reasonable explanation. To demonstrate this, let us consider the writings of William A. Cox:

> The communion is *not a mere form.* It is *more than a memorial.* I believe God has given us the fellowship of the holy communion so that we may draw nigh to Him, and not only draw nigh but also receive from Him the supply of our every need.

He continues by rejecting the doctrines of consubstantiation and transubstantiation, and says, "We believe it is a memorial, a symbol." He seems to be struggling to properly express his view. But then he begins to associate participation in Holy Communion with the indwelling of Jesus Christ and baptism in the Holy Spirit, and his language regarding the "symbols" of the meal becomes very sacramental.

It (the Lord's Supper) is not an empty service, it does not mean simply being served with a little bread and wine on the first Sunday of the month—it is a means of fellowship with God, through Jesus, by the Spirit, and we have a right to come to it expecting God to meet us. Indeed we have a right to expect to draw so near to God that whatever our need may be at that moment, whether spiritual or physical, He will supply it . . . when we eat of the divine body of the Lord Jesus, the living Bread which came down from heaven . . . He quickens the spiritual man; He revives the physical; He heals our diseases, and gives us strength to live by. By eating Jesus, the Bread of life, we have life in our physical bodies . . . if we eat the flesh of Jesus, and drink His blood, we shall live by Him. So when you want to be healed, just take a great big meal of Jesus.

Communion is not a dead, traditional rite. To partake of the holy meal is transformative — "the very nature of the individual is changed . . . strengthened and empowered by the very life and body of the Lord Jesus Christ" (WE, 4 May 1918). Believers were encouraged, ". . . while we are taking Communion, let us get into the Spirit and draw from God" (PE, 25 May 1929). Faith is experiential and an experiential faith is accompanied by spiritual manifestations that may be perceived by the physical senses. Cecil Knight, a Pentecostal leader of a later generation, wrote that the observance of Holy Communion should be a "vital part of the church's life in worshiping the Risen Christ." Knight believed the bread and cup are more than symbols. He wrote:

There is deep spiritual meaning in the Lord's Supper. The participant does *not merely look at the symbols; he receives spiritual food.* Just as the bread and the fruit of the vine will *nourish and invigorate* the body of man, so Christ, through Communion, *sustains and quickens* the soul. When a Christian truly worships Christ in the Lord's Supper, he is ministered to by the Holy Spirit, thereby receiving strength and a deep abiding peace (COGE, 22 Mar 1971).

In Holy Communion there is a real presence — Christ and Spirit — whose presence in the celebration are a means of grace — sustenance, strength, and peace.

The Trinitarian administration of salvation is reflected in a Pentecostal understanding of the holy meal. In the *way of salvation*, the work of the Son and the Spirit are complimentary and interdependent. The believer encounters one through the activity of the other. According to Hebrews, Christ our High Priest offered Himself as a spotless sacrifice to God "through the eternal Spirit" (Heb. 9:14). The bread and cup of the Lord's Supper are gifts of Christ through the Spirit. The Lord's Supper is possible only by virtue of Pentecost. The Spirit makes Christ present in the bread and cup. Pentecostals gladly affirm the presence of Christ and the witness of the Spirit in the worshiping community. With emphasis on the miraculous, it seems logical that Pentecostals would be willing to affirm the presence of Christ and the Spirit in the bread and cup of the holy meal. These two views are not mutually exclusive.

THE MEDICINE OF IMMORTALITY

In the Gospel of Matthew, we find that the feeding miracles are performed in the context of Jesus' healing ministry. The first feeding miracle and the miracle of Jesus walking on the water occur between Matthew's reporting of Jesus healing the sick. Just before the feeding miracle, Jesus "saw a large crowd, and felt compassion for them and healed their sick" (Matt. 14:14). Immediately after Jesus walked on the water, He and His disciples arrived at Gennesaret where "the men of that place recognized

Him, they sent word into all that surrounding district and brought to Him all who were sick; and they implored Him that they might just touch the fringe of His cloak; and as many as touched it were cured" (Matt. 14:35-36). Likewise, the second feeding miracle at the Sea of Galilee occurred in the context of Jesus' healing ministry (Matt. 15:29-38). In both feeding miracles, Jesus was concerned for the well-being of the multitudes. He was moved with compassion and concerned that the people might faint, or grow weary, for their lack of sustenance. Also, in both instances, Jesus commanded His disciples to feed the multitude, and Jesus offered a blessing and a prayer of thanksgiving for the loaves and fishes (Matt. 14:19). In healing the sick and providing food for the weary, Jesus was restoring peace to the people of God. Jesus is the Anointed One who restores and satisfies the sick and hungry. Citing the prophet Isaiah, Matthew wrote:

> When evening came, they brought to Him many who were demon-possessed; and He cast out the spirits with a word, and healed all who were ill. This was to fulfill what was spoken through Isaiah the prophet: "He Himself took our infirmities and carried away our diseases" (Matt. 8:16-17).

Jesus' healing miracles were signs of the coming of the kingdom of God in which the powers of sin and death are destroyed. Healing miracles are not an end unto themselves. They are signs that point to the resurrection of the dead. In both feeding miracles, Jesus blessed the meal and then gave the loaves and fishes to His disciples for distribution to the multitudes. Later, when Jesus gathered His disciples to share His last Passover meal, He gave thanks for the bread and cup and passed the bread and cup to His disciples.

> While they were eating, Jesus took some bread, and after a blessing, He broke it and gave it to the disciples, and said, "Take, eat; this is My body." And when He had taken a cup and given thanks, He gave it to them, saying, "Drink from it, all of you; for this is My blood of the covenant, which is poured out for many for forgiveness of sins" (Matt. 26:26-28).

This meal, the Lord's Supper, is offered for the salvation of humanity. This is the ultimate feeding miracle in which Jesus has offered His own body on the cross, and in the bread and cup, for human salvation.

An ancient theologian referred to the bread of the Lord's Supper as the "medicine of immortality, the antidote we take in order not to die, but to live forever in Jesus Christ." All humans suffer from a terminal disease—sin. Because of our sinfulness, we are corrupt. This corruption is demonstrated in a multitude of diseases — physical, psychological, and spiritual. The early church believed that by partaking in the Lord's Supper, believers receive "medicine" that heals. In the bread and cup of the Lord's Supper, believers partake of the flesh and blood of the Great Physician. The healing ministry of Christ continues through the holy meal.

Early Pentecostals enthusiastically affirmed the ancient understanding of the Lord's Supper as therapeutic – a healing meal. Actually, it is here in associating the Lord's Supper with divine healing that Pentecostals completely embraced the holy meal as a sacrament—a means of grace in which Christ is present.

> The Lord Jesus is brought very near in the observance of the Lord's Supper. The redemptive work for the body is often attested to, as the communicants partake in faith, drinking His blood, and eating His flesh, the Lord healing them of sicknesses and delivering them of infirmities. Praise His precious name forever (WW, Aug 1915).

This theme is common in the writings of early Pentecostals, and continues to be present among many Pentecostals today. The Lord's Supper is often presented as a means of grace that has a twofold purpose. The cup represents the blood of Jesus Christ which is shed for the remission of sins. The broken bread represents the body of the Lord, which was broken for the healing of the physical body. Pentecostals often referred to the Lord's Supper as "God's medicine." It was suggested that some believers left the Lord's Table sick and afflicted because they did not properly discern "in the bread His perfect body broken for their imperfect bodies." Early Pentecostal periodicals included testimonies of believers who were healed as they participated in the Lord's Supper. Pentecostal Communion services are not to be mere ritual. They are gracious encounters with God in which believers are brought into God's presence so that they may receive spiritual nourishment for their souls and medicine for their physical bodies.

PROPHETIC WORSHIP

The celebration of the Lord's Supper is a prophetic act of worship. The active presence of Spirit in worship is at the heart of Pentecostal belief and practice. As worshipers sing and pray, and as the Spirit is manifested in worship, there may be shouts of praise, expressive dancing, and/or ecstatic tongues. When sinners are present, the Holy Spirit "convicts" or "confronts" with a call to repentance. Worshipers experiencing the presence of God, identify with the prophet Isaiah, who cried, "Woe is me, for I am ruined! Because I am a man of unclean lips, and I live among a people of unclean lips; for my eyes have seen the King, the Lord of hosts" (Isaiah 6:5). The apostle Paul experienced a sense of the same as he wrote, "But if all prophesy, and an unbeliever or an ungifted man enters, he is convicted by all, he is called to account by all; the secrets of his heart are disclosed; and so he will fall on his face and worship God, declaring that God is certainly among you" (1 Cor. 14:24-25). The presence of God in worship is a prophetic call whereby sins are disclosed, sinners are convicted, and God is exalted. In the same manner, celebration of the Lord's Supper is a prophetic act of worship. When instructing the Corinthians regarding proper observance of the Lord's Supper, Paul speaks of spiritual accountability.

> Therefore whoever eats the bread or drinks the cup of the Lord in an unworthy manner, shall be guilty of the body and the blood of the Lord. But a man must examine himself, and in so doing he is to eat of the bread and drink of the

cup. For he who eats and drinks, eats and drinks judgment to himself if he does not judge the body rightly. For this reason many among you are weak and sick, and a number sleep. But if we judged ourselves rightly, we would not be judged. But when we are judged, we are disciplined by the Lord so that we will not be condemned along with the world (1 Cor. 11:27-32).

Self-examination and the discipline of the Lord are integral aspects of sacramental worship. It is through self-examination that worshipers escape the Lord's discipline and judgment. When Isaiah stood at the temple altar, he became intensely aware of personal sins. Similarly, when a publican prostrated himself before God, he accurately discerned his spiritual deficiency (Luke 18:13). Both Isaiah and the publican encountered God's holiness, discerned their sinfulness, and experienced the grace and power of God. This self-examination takes place within the worshiping community before the Lord's Table. There is an element of accountability to other worshipers. The Scriptures are replete with examples of those who discerned their spiritual condition incorrectly and encountered the discipline and judgment of the Lord. Judgment begins at the "household of God" (1 Peter 4:17). The boastful Pharisee trusted his own righteousness, and was not justified before God (Luke 18:11). Ananias and Sapphira discovered too late they could not hide sin from the discerning Spirit and suffered swift judgment (Acts 5:1-11). To be "in covenant" with God means that individuals present themselves in accountability to the whole body. Paul commanded the Corinthians to discipline those in the church guilty of immorality, lest the whole church suffer the judgment of one person's sin. The Table of the Lord can be a place where the Spirit reveals sin and thus brings the guilty to repentance. Anyone who approaches the Table of the Lord unrepentant, or irreverently, risks the Table of Life becoming a table of death. The purpose of such discipline and judgment is redemptive. The hope is that the offending one might be saved (1 Cor. 5:1-5; 11:32; Heb. 12:5-11; Rev. 3:19). When approaching the Lord's Table, a worshiper who fails to self-judge correctly will be judged by the sovereign Lord. An ancient sage warned, "Guard your steps as you go to the house of God and draw near to listen rather than to offer the sacrifice of fools; for they do not know they are doing evil" (Ecclesiastes 5:1). However, Paul does not state that sinful individuals should be refused the Table of Lord, but that everyone who approaches the Lord's Table should do so with great care. The Table of the Lord, as a means of grace, is a place where the Spirit reveals sin and brings the guilty to repentance. The church should never refuse grace to a sinner who comes to the Table.

The Lord's Supper is a meal of confession and reconciliation. As believers approach the Table of the Lord, they must come in unbroken fellowship. Sometimes this requires times of private and public confession. Relationships within family and church cannot be healed without sincere confession. The issue is holiness—a holy church that offers holy worship. Jesus said, "Therefore you are to be perfect, as your heavenly Father is perfect" (Matt. 5:48). Paul encouraged, "Let us cleanse ourselves from all defilement of flesh and spirit, perfecting holiness in the fear of God" (2 Cor. 7:1). Each believer must strive for perfection. When sinfulness is discovered, the only remedy is confession. The Christian church must be a holy fellowship. Quarrels within the fellowship demonstrate the presence of lust and greed (James 4:1-2). Jesus is coming for "a glorious church, not having spot or wrinkle or any such thing, but that she should be holy and without blemish" (Eph. 5:27). The Lord's Supper offers an opportunity for believers to examine their own lives, as well and the spiritual health of the community. As the church gathers around the altar, or Table of the Lord, sinful believers may come seeking mercy. We must understand that sincere confession is not a license to sin. Confession is placing ourselves under subjection to spiritual elders who will offer prayers on our behalf as well as hold us accountable. Confession is not an excuse for sin, but seeking deliverance from sin. This is often a painful process and many tears will be shed, but the outcome is joy and eternal life.

The Lord's Supper anticipates the Marriage Supper of the Lamb (Rev. 19:9). Paul said, "For as often as you eat this bread and drink the cup, you proclaim the Lord's death *until He comes*" (1 Cor. 11:26). The return of Christ is the blessed hope of the church (Titus 2:13). The resurrection of the body is the hope of every Christian (1 Cor. 15:16-19). At the Table of the Lord, believers participate in a meal that anticipates the resurrection of the body and the new heaven and earth. The bread and cup of Christ express the deepest hopes of humanity. Pentecostalism is a last-days movement. The outpouring of the Holy Spirit and the renewal of spiritual gifts are prophetic signs that God has inaugurated the "last days." Pentecostals anticipate the imminent return of the Lord. Because of the last-days emphasis in Pentecostal theology, celebration of the Lord's Supper should be a primary element of Pentecostal worship.

SACRAMENT OF UNITY

The celebration of the Lord's Supper calls the church to unity with Christ. Paul's criticism of the Corinthians was directed at disorderly worship and relational divisions. The first issue Paul addressed was their division (1 Cor. 1:10-13). The Corinthian church was divided over issues regarding spiritual authority, and other social, cultural, and economic issues. The Corinthian church consisted of Jews and Gentiles, rich and poor, slave and free. Their diversity, which should have been a testimony to the power of the gospel to heal social brokenness, violated the very purpose of their gathering. Instead of demonstrating unity in Christ, the Lord's Supper became a reflection of the brokenness of their fellowship. Paul's rebuke was harsh: "You come together not for the better, but for the worse . . . Do you despise the church of God?" (1 Cor. 11:17, 22). To Paul, a broken and divided church is an offense to the reconciling power of the cross and an offense to the body and blood of Christ in the Lord's Supper (1 Cor. 1:11-18; 11:27). His rebuke was a call to unity that demonstrates the transformative power of the gospel that heals the brokenness of human community.

The unity of the church is demonstrated in that all Christians are in fellowship with a singular Bishop — the Lord Jesus Christ (1 Peter 2:25; 5:4). The unity of the church must be an expression of devotion to Jesus Christ as Lord and His command that believers are to love one another. Those who share the common confession that "Jesus is Lord" and embrace a common encounter in the Holy Spirit should lead the effort to bring all believers together at the Lord's Table in the unity of the Holy Spirit. A first generation Pentecostal, G. F. Taylor, understood the significance of the Lord's Supper. He wrote, "The real purpose of the Supper is to humiliate us, to teach us the spirit of Jesus, and to unite us as a church in the spirit of fellowship" (PHA, 10 Jul 1919).

CELEBRATION OF THE LORD'S SUPPER

The Lord's Supper was a normative event celebrated weekly, or perhaps, daily in the early church. The challenge for Pentecostal pastors is to integrate the celebration of the Lord's Supper into regular worship in a way that encourages worshipers to encounter the Holy Spirit. For Pentecostals, worship is defined as a "Spirit-movement" and is expressed in terms of movement — the lifting of hands, clapping, shouting, dancing, and many other physical activities. One of the most significant movements in the Pentecostal worship service is the altar call. As the Holy Spirit moves during worship, Pentecostal worshipers are encouraged to move to the altar. Hence, it is natural for Pentecostals to respond to an invitation to come to the altar to receive the Lord's Supper. This was the preferred method of many first-generation Pentecostals.

> On Saturday night, July 30, after the sermon by Brother Latimer, *the saints assembled at the altar for the sacrament*, afterwards came the good old time love feast of feet washing (COGE, 20 Aug 1921).

The Lord's Supper should be celebrated as an altar call where worshipers present themselves as "a living sacrifice, holy, acceptable to God" (Rom. 12:1) and receive the body and blood of Jesus. There is evidence to suggest that ancient observances of the Lord's Supper included spontaneous moves of the Holy Spirit. The Apostle Paul associates the blessing over the Lord's Supper with "praying in the Spirit" (1 Cor. 14:16-17). If the celebration of Holy Communion is to be a Spirit movement, pastors and congregations should nurture the expectation that these services are Spirit-empowered events. Remember, movement to the altar is the heart of Pentecostal worship. Through the years, I have observed many believers as they approached the altar to receive the holy meal. Many people who don't frequently respond to an altar call will come to receive the Lord's Supper. As they come to the Table they do so prayerfully and reverently. They move to the altar with the other faithful believers. Often they tarry at the altar prayerfully reflecting upon the significance of the Lord's Supper. They come to the altar, not to receive the bread and cup, but to encounter God through Christ and the Spirit. This is a faithful expression of Pentecostal spirituality. Consider the following reflection from the Church of God *Book of Doctrines*:

> Those who have not participated in the service of the Lord's Supper have missed some of the most sacred and hallowed moments in the entire Christian Life. The heart melts completely in contemplation of the death and suffering of Christ. In deep contrition, and repeated regret that our hearts could ever have been so far away from Him, we beg and implore, Father, forgive us our trespasses as we forgive those who trespass against us. Usually the heart is softened in the deepest gratitude and devotion, and often we break into tears. When we think how Christ suffered in His agonizing prayer in Gethsemane, our sorrow is often too deep for tears. Surely nothing could take the place of the Lord's Supper. As the unleavened bread is broken can we not hear the beat of the hammer that drove the nails into His hands and His feet? And the spear piercing His side? And as we behold the wine in the cup, does it not better than anything else in the world bring thoughts of the shed blood of Christ- the tears in the Garden that were as great drops of blood? And the blood that trickled down,

and flowed from His hands and His feet, and gushed from His side and He bowed His head, and said, "It is finished." May the day not come when we shall forget Calvary and the sacrifice for sin that was made there for the whole world. And could that include even me? It could, and that is the thought that fills our heart as we partake of the body and blood of the Lord is symbol and remembrance until He comes. Even so come Lord Jesus.

6

FOOT-WASHING

THE FELLOWSHIP OF THE TOWEL

Jesus, knowing that the Father had given all things into His hands, and that He had come forth from God and was going back to God, got up from supper, and laid aside His garments; and taking a towel, He girded Himself. Then He poured water into the basin, and began to wash the disciples' feet and to wipe them with the towel with which He was girded . . .

So when He had washed their feet, and taken His garments and reclined at the table again, He said to them, "Do you know what I have done to you? "You call Me Teacher and Lord; and you are right, for so I am. If I then, the Lord and the Teacher, washed your feet, you also ought to wash one another's feet. For I gave you an example that you also should do as I did to you (John 13:3-5; 12-15).

Foot-washing is a sacred act of worship that has a special significance in my spiritual journey. Foot-washing is the Spirit and church at play. Foot-washing services are joyful occasions in which believers express love and devotion for each other. Believers wash each other's feet as they shout, pray, and speak in other tongues. In the midst of this symphony of praise, one can hear the sounds of water splashing. At times, it all seems a bit silly, like watching small children play under the water hose during a hot summer day. Maybe the appeal of foot-washing is that as we come to "play in the Spirit," we become little children. By participating in foot-washing, our pretense is stripped away. One may walk into a foot-washing service as a respected attorney or professor, but in moments, the pretense of respected position is erased as believers worship in their bare feet, washing the feet of their brothers in Christ.

Foot-washing as a sacred act of worship demonstrates such loving service. Throughout the history of the church, foot-washing has often been adopted by renewal movements. For many Pentecostal churches, the sacrament of foot-washing has been significant to congregational spirituality and worship. W. J. Seymour listed foot-washing as one of the "three ordinances of the church." For Seymour, foot-washing was a "type of regeneration" and was an act of devotion that led the participants to "humility and charity" (AF, Sep 1907). The first General Assembly of the Church of God declared that "Communion and feet washing are taught by the New Testament Scriptures . . . [therefore] in order to preserve the unity of the body, and to obey the sacred Word, we recommend that every member engage in these sacred services . . . one or more times each year" (BM). Foot-washing is one of the "sacred services" of the Church, ordained by the Scriptures. "Every member" is encouraged to observe this sacred service on the basis of fidelity to the "sacred Word" and the unity of the church. Also, even though the official statement suggests that foot-washing be observed "one or more times each year" it was observed much more frequently. Foot-washing was observed at revivals, camp meetings, and special services. A. J. Tomlinson wrote:

> The feet washing service is one among the most beautiful and attractive services that we have. To see a little crowd of devoted saints humbly bowing before one another in holy reverence to Jesus and performing this little service just because Jesus said we ought to do it, and does not explain or give the reason for it, it is a mark of devotion and sincerity worthy of the most commendatory remarks . . . There may be something deeper in feet washing than we will ever know in this world (COGE, 5 May 1917).

Judging from the early literature, it can be faithfully stated that foot-washing was just as important to the spirituality of these early Pentecostals as was speaking in tongues.

THE DESCENT OF THE ETERNAL WORD

The Gospel of John presents a high Christology. Jesus Christ is the eternal Word who assumed human flesh. There is no ambiguity in John's claims about Jesus. The descent and incarnation of the eternal Word is summarized in just a few words: "And the Word became flesh, and dwelt among us, and we saw His glory, glory as of the only begotten from the Father, full of grace and truth" (John 1:14). John declared that God the Word descended from the glory and power essential to His nature to assume our nature and dwell among us. The descent of the Lord is a theme common to the New Testament. Peter spoke of the descent of our Lord when he "made proclamation to the spirits now in prison" (1 Peter 3:19). In a beautiful early hymn of the church, Paul relates to us the heart of his Christology:

> . . . Christ Jesus, who, although He existed in the form of God, did not regard equality with God a thing to be grasped, but *emptied Himself, taking the form of a bond-servant,* and being made in the likeness of men. Being found in appearance as a man, *He humbled Himself* by becoming obedient to the point of death, even death on a cross. For this reason also, God highly exalted Him, and bestowed on Him the name which is above every name, so that at the name of Jesus every knee will bow, of those who are in heaven and on earth and under the earth, and that every tongue will confess that Jesus Christ is Lord, to the glory of God the Father (Philip. 2:5-11).

The apostolic witness of the New Testament interprets the Incarnation using terms denoting humility and service. The image of Jesus rising from the table, laying aside His garments, taking a towel, pouring water into a basin, bowing before His disciples and washing their feet incorporates into one prophetic action the significance of the Incarnation. The story of Jesus washing the feet of His disciples serves as the introduction to the story of His impending death on the cross, which is the climax of the Word's descent. Jesus said, "I am the good shepherd; the good shepherd lays down His life for the sheep . . . No one has taken it away from Me, but I lay it down on my own initiative" (John 10:11, 18). In Christ's own self-emptying He has revealed to us the glory of God.

Christians are called to emptiness, humility, self-denial, and voluntary poverty. This is the spirituality of foot-washing — the fellowship of the towel. This is a difficult spirituality for Christians who live in a culture of affluence, where spirituality is defined in terms of prosperity and success. One who wishes to enter into the fellowship of the towel must first experience the emptying of one's self. When a rich young ruler came to Jesus seeking eternal life, he was told to empty himself. Jesus said, "One thing you still lack; sell all that you possess and distribute it to the poor, and you shall have treasure in heaven; and come, follow Me" (Luke 18:22). When Peter confessed, "You are the Christ," Jesus told His disciples "If anyone wishes to come after Me, he must deny himself, and take up his cross and follow Me" (Mark 8:34). Paul challenged the believers at Philippi: "Do nothing from selfishness or empty conceit, but with humility of mind regard one another as more important than yourselves" (Philip. 2:3). Foot-washing is more than a sacramental act of worship; it is a way of life. As a sacrament, participation in foot-washing is to participate in the humiliation of our Lord.

CHRIST'S SACRIFICIAL DEATH

Foot-washing interprets Christ's sacrificial death. One of the major distinctions between John's Gospel and the synoptic Gospels is that of the relationship between the Lord's Supper as presented in the synoptic gospels, and the foot-washing as presented by John.

The three synoptic Gospels relate the institution of the Lord's Supper in conjunction with the Passover (Matt. 26:17-19; Mark 14:12-16; Luke 22:7-13). John presents the foot-washing in conjunction with the Passover. The foot-washing story is not presented by John in order to replace the Lord's Supper, but as an interpretation it. Both the Lord's Supper and Jesus' washing of his disciples' feet are presented as redemptive events by the collective witness of the four Gospels. In the synoptic Gospels, Jesus offered bread and wine — His body and blood — to establish the covenant of salvation. In John, Jesus washed the feet of His disciples so that they might be cleansed and be in fellowship with Him (John 13:8-10). In the synoptic Gospels, the Lord's Supper anticipates the cross and represents Christ's sacrificial death. In the gospel of John, Jesus' washing of His disciples' feet interprets the cross as the climax of the Son's descent in service to humanity.

The foot-washing event is presented in terms of Christ's saving love and death. It is a regenerative act in that as Jesus washed their feet, the disciples experienced a spiritual transformation. Unless the disciples allowed Jesus to wash their feet, they could have "no part" of Him (John 13:8). The significance of this event as redemptive cannot be discounted. For Christ's disciples, foot-washing was not a matter of their individual consciences, but a matter of salvation. To have their feet washed by Jesus was to confess Him as "Teacher and Lord" (John 13:13). Also, Jesus commanded His disciples to wash one another's feet (John 13:14). By doing so, they affirmed each other as disciples of Jesus. Foot-washing interprets the cross as Jesus having laid down His life for His disciples. Likewise, He commanded His disciples to lay down their lives for one another.

SANCTIFICATION

The Gospel of John does not present an explicit account of Jesus' baptism, nor does John present the institution of the Lord's Supper. However, water baptism and the Lord's Supper serve as redemptive themes throughout. John presents Jesus washing His disciples' feet and His corresponding command that they wash each other's feet in the theological context of baptism and the Lord's Supper. Foot-washing interprets the Lord's Supper in terms of the descent of the Son and His sacrificial death. Foot-washing compliments water baptism and signifies the ongoing life of faith.

Foot-washing is not the initial regenerative event and should not be confused with water baptism. John presented water baptism as the first of the transformation rituals (John 3:3, 5). Foot-washing is presented as a subsequent event which indicates a continuing relationship in which the believer moves from being a new convert to a bond-servant of the Lord. Whereas, water baptism is presented as a single, initial event corresponding to the new birth; foot-washing is presented as an oft-repeated event corresponding to the believer's need of continual cleansing. The conversation between Jesus and Peter reflects the distinction between water baptism and foot-washing:

> Peter said to Him, "Never shall You wash my feet!" Jesus answered him, "If I do not wash you, you have no part with Me." Simon Peter said to Him, "Lord, then wash not only my feet, but also my hands and my head." Jesus said to him, "He who has bathed needs only to wash his feet" (John 13:8-10).

The "bath" to which the Lord refers may be that of water baptism. Peter has made his confession of faith and has been "born of water and the Spirit." That which Peter and the disciples now require is not the initial bath of cleansing, but a subsequent cleansing. Jesus desires that His disciples be "completely clean" (John 13:10).

Pentecostals have taught that sinners must "bear fruits in keeping with repentance" (Luke 3:8; 19:8-9). Repentance of fallen believers includes doing one's "first works" (Rev. 2:5). The Pentecostal *way of salvation* is the pursuit of holiness, which is, sharing in the moral excellence of God. The pursuit of holiness affects the whole human self—spirit, soul, and body. Therefore, the confession of sin includes a right disposition of the heart, a true confession of the mouth, and presenting the body as "a living and holy sacrifice, acceptable to God, which is your spiritual service of worship" (Rom. 12:1).

Foot-washing is a sacramental act that by the power of the Holy Spirit effects sanctification within the Christian community. Foot-washing is an expression of profound love and humility which offers an opportunity for the sinful to confess their offenses and receive forgiveness. James wrote, "Therefore, confess your sins to one another, and pray for one another so that you may be healed" (James 5:16). Too often, we have viewed confession of sin as a private matter—a matter of concern between the sinner and the Lord only. This individualistic view of repentance too often allows the sinful Christian to hide behind a false grace. This false grace becomes a license to sin, and sinfulness is not remedied. If the purpose of confession and forgiveness is juridical only, that is, a divine declaration of pardon, then this "Jesus-and-me" religion will suffice. However, according to James, the confession of sin "to one another" is significant to healing and restoration to wholeness. Secret sin often leads to personal anguish. The psalmist prayed, "When I kept silent about my sin, my body wasted away through my groaning all day long" (Psalm 32:3).

The ultimate purpose of confession is sanctification. This means that the sinful Christian must tell the truth about oneself. Instead of hiding behind a false sense of grace, the penitent believer reveals oneself and is transformed by grace. This type of confession and forgiveness of sin takes place within the community of faith. The regular confession of sin in the presence of one's brothers and sisters offers an opportunity for the cleansing of guilt and sorrow. The sinner must seek forgiveness from and reconciliation with the offended individuals (Matt. 5:23-24). The church graciously responds and offers forgiveness. This is signified in foot-washing.

Foot-washing is a ministry of the high priestly office of Christ. The writer of Hebrews tells us that the priesthood of Jesus Christ is "eternal" and "unchangeable" and that "He always lives to make intercession" for His disciples (Heb. 7:24-25). Within the community of Jesus' disciples, there had been a clash of egos and many examples of failure. The disciples found themselves ineffective in exorcising a demon. Jesus rebuked them for their faithlessness (Mark 9:17-19). James and John sought power, to be first in the Kingdom. This desire led to contention among the

Twelve (Mark 10:35-41). Even as Peter confessed, "You are the Christ," he rebuked the Lord. Later, after insisting "I will never fall away," he denied that he knew the Lord three times (Matt. 16:12-22; 26:69-75). Judas betrayed the Lord (Matt. 26:47-49). As high priest, Jesus washed the feet of all His disciples in spite of their failures. He washed their feet *because* of their failures, so they might be cleansed of sin.

The *way of salvation* begins with repentance and water baptism. Foot-washing is a means of grace for subsequent cleansing. The Spirit, who graces the waters of baptism, also graces the waters of foot-washing. Water baptism represents new birth, regeneration, and initial cleansing. Foot-washing signifies the continuous cleansing of sanctification that is necessary for Christians who live in this corrupt age. This is affirmed in the testimony of early Pentecostals. In a report from a Church of God convention in Alabama, H. G. Rogers wrote:

> We surely had a good time. God was with us in giving out the word. Some were saved and some were blest in a wonderful way. On Sunday the saints met and partook of the Lord's Supper and washed feet. The Holy Ghost manifested Himself in a wonderful way. *One man was sanctified just after his feet were washed.* O, how it pays to obey God and be happy. On Monday there were twenty who followed the Lord in baptism. The Lord wonderfully blest them (COGE, 1 Jun 1910).

Foot-washing reminds us that the church is a community of grace where sinful Christians are to be welcomed and restored. Jesus commanded that His disciples wash one another's feet. The disciples of Jesus can be a contentious group. Because each believer is "in Christ," a member of the one body of Christ, the one who washes the feet of another, does so as an extension of Christ the high priest. In other words, to have our feet washed by a brother or sister in Christ is to have our feet washed vicariously by Christ.

A New Commandment

> A new commandment I give to you, that you love one another, even as I have loved you, that you also love one another. By this all men will know that you are My disciples, if you have love for one another (John 13:35).

Foot-washing is a rite that signifies following after Jesus, living a life of self-denial, and expressing divine love. The new commandment is not incidental to the foot-washing episode, but essential to it. By washing the feet of his disciples, the Beloved Son has exemplified God's love to humanity and has demonstrated to his disciples a new way of being the people of God.

For many, love is something experienced and felt. Love can be romantic, even erotic, and is expressed sexually. Love can also be familial, that is, the love expressed within a family or within a friendship. The most common form of love in the New Testament is expressed as *agape*. This word is rarely used in ancient Greek literature, but it is the most common word for love in the New Testament. Why? Jesus Christ redefined the notion of love. There was no popular Greek word which could fully express Christian love, so the early Christian writers appropriated and redefined *agape* for their own use. The pagan notions of love emphasize pleasure. Ancient Christians were not opposed to pleasure associated with love, but they were opposed to the notion of love solely for the sake of pleasure. Instead, *agape* denotes the self-sacrifical, self-giving nature of love. *Agape* is not the popular notion of "unconditional love," but love that is conditioned by the redemptive purpose of God. *Agape* is the choice to give of oneself, to deny oneself, even to empty oneself for the sake of the beloved. This love is the essence of God (1 John 4:8) and the action of God (John 3:16). This love is also the proper human response to God (Luke 10:27). To "love the Lord your God with all your" heart, life, strength, and mind suggest that the "Who" and "how" of the loving response are significant. The "Who" is revealed to us through the Incarnation and Pentecost, both of which are self-giving acts of

God. The "how" of our loving response to God suggests that we offer our lives (body, heart, and head) as a "living and holy sacrifice" in service to God and to God's people (Rom.12:1).

The regenerative and sanctifying act of foot-washing signifies the transformation of love, that is, the foot-washing event redefines love through the acts of Christ. Whereas the pagan notion of *erotic* love tends to objectify others for the sake of the lovers' self-pleasure; the Christian notion of *agape* converts the heart so that the lover seeks the well-being of the loved. Even when speaking of the marital love, the apostles preferred the word *agape*.

> Husbands, love your wives, just as Christ also loved the church and gave Himself up for her, so that He might *sanctify* her, having *cleansed* her by the washing of water with the word, that He might present to Himself the church in all her glory, having no spot or wrinkle or any such thing; but that she would be holy and blameless. So husbands ought also to love their own wives as their own bodies. He who loves his own wife loves himself; for no one ever hated his own flesh, but *nourishes and cherishes* it, just as Christ also does the church, because we are members of His body (Eph. 5:25-30).

Paul speaks of marital love as a great mystery "with reference to Christ and the church" (Eph. 5:32). The church is the bride of Christ and the love that unites the church is characterized by the words sanctify, cleansed, nourish, and cherish. Within the bridal party love is expressed as mutual submission to the needs of the other (Eph. 5:21). In ancient Jewish, Greek, and Roman homes the wife lived in servitude to her husband. The nature of *agape* upends that arrangement. By washing his disciples' feet, Jesus demonstrated that in God's family the bride-groom is the servant of the bride, the bride-groom sanctifies the bride, and nourishes and cherishes the bride. Jesus said,

> For I gave you an example that you also should do as I did to you. Truly, truly, I say to you, a slave is not greater than his master, nor is one who is sent greater than the one who

sent him. If you know these things, you are blessed if you do them (John 13:15-17).

Foot-washing as profound act of humility is not an expression of low self-esteem, but the action of one who understands power and authority and is willing to sacrifice it for the well-being of others. The Apostle Peter encourages the followers of Jesus: "For you have been called for this purpose, since Christ also suffered for you, leaving you an example for you to follow in His steps" (1 Peter 2:21). The followers of Jesus will "suffer for the sake of righteousness" (1 Peter 3:14). Christian love is exemplified in the joyful willingness to embrace a life of suffering for the sake of the healing of humanity.

AUTHENTIC CHRISTIAN MINISTRY

Foot-washing exemplifies authentic Christian ministry. Jesus said, "Truly, truly, I say to you, he who receives whomever I send receives Me; and he who receives Me receives Him who sent Me" (Jn. 13:20). The foot-washing of the disciples is performed in the context of their apostolic mission. Jesus is the Divine Servant, the disciples are servants of the Divine One, and as such are servants to the world. The apostle Paul twice used the metaphor of "feet" to speak of the proclamation of the gospel (Rom. 10:15; Eph. 6:15). The apostolic vestments of Christian service include shoes of peace and a garment of humility (Eph. 6:15; 1 Peter 5:5). In speaking of the "body of Christ," Paul tells us that the church is comprised of many parts. Christ is the head of the body (Eph. 5:23). As the head of the church, through the Holy Spirit, Christ has given to the church various ministries—apostles, prophets, pastors, teachers, evangelists; and various offices—deacon and bishop (1 Cor. 12:28; Eph. 4:11). These ministries and offices are the feet of the body. Christ as the head oversees and guides His church. The ministers and officers of the church carry the body and move the body under the direction of Christ.

Among the greatest temptations for humans is that of power and authority. Power intoxicates and corrupts the human soul. One would hope that those who serve the church would not be so easily seduced, but we know that we are not immune. The first-century Corinthian church suffered from schism and turmoil. Many people within the church challenged and rejected the apostolic ministry of Paul. The leaders of this group were known as "the super-apostles." Much of the conflict between Paul and the super-apostles was due to their models of ministry. Paul's model of ministry was that of "weakness" and the "meekness and gentleness of Christ" (1 Cor. 2:3; 2 Cor. 10:1). The model of the super-apostles was that of triumphalism. The super-apostles commended themselves as men of divine power and boasted in their charismatic gifts. However, Paul was "unimpressive" and his preaching style was "contemptible" (2 Cor. 10:10; 11:6). Paul's ministry was characterized by "weakness and fear," and he suffered from many bodily ailments, one of which was a "thorn in the flesh, a messenger of Satan" (1 Cor. 2:3; 2 Cor. 12:7: Gal. 4:3). When the members of the Corinthian church compared the two models of ministry before them, they favored the super-apostles. However, with all the apparent strengths of the super-apostles they lacked that which is necessary to establish an authentic Christian ministry, that is, a model of ministry that follows after the example of Jesus Christ. In fact, they were not super-apostles, but false apostles (2 Cor. 11:13-15).

Authentic Christian ministry is not defined simply in terms of bold, charismatic leadership. Christian ministry is best defined in the willingness to lay all garments aside, and take up the towel and basin to wash the feet of God's people. Foot-washing exemplifies authentic Christian ministry in that by participation in this sacrament, we embrace Christ's sufferings for the sake of the church. With Paul, we may proclaim, "Now I rejoice in my sufferings for your sake, and in my flesh I do my share on behalf of His body, which is the church, in filling up what is lacking in Christ's afflictions" (Col. 1:24).

WASHING JESUS' FEET

There are two texts that speak of Jesus' feet being washed: Luke 7:36-45 and John 12:1-8. In these stories, two women demonstrate their love for Jesus. Both events are interpreted as redemptive. In John, Mary, the sister of Lazarus, anointed the feet of Jesus with perfume and wiped them with her hair. Mary was a righteous woman, a devoted disciple. She was accustomed to sitting at the Lord's feet and listening to His teaching. Once Jesus said, "Mary has chosen the good part, which shall not be taken away from her" (Luke 10:42). Her act of devotion filled the house with the fragrance of the perfume. Judas was offended by the extravagance of her gesture. But his offense was that of a distracted disciple who was unaware of the significance of the event he had witnessed. This occurred just before the Passover and was interpreted as preparation for the burial of the crucified Lord. In John 13, Jesus washed the feet of His disciples so that they might be cleansed and have life in Him. Among all of His disciples, only Mary had the prophetic insight to anticipate Jesus' self-sacrifice as the Lamb of God. She anointed and washed the feet that would carry our Lord to the cross.

In Luke, a prostitute anointed the feet of Jesus with expensive perfume, washed his feet with her tears, and wiped them with her hair. Simon the Pharisee was offended by her presence in his home. Jesus was not offended; He is the friend of sinners. The Lord responded to her gesture of devotion with forgiveness: "Your sins are forgiven . . . Your faith has saved you. Go in peace" (Luke 7:48, 50).

Foot-washing signifies the restoration of the sinful. Christ identifies Himself with the stranger, the poor, the hungry, and the prisoner. He is the friend of sinners. When Christ returns in the power and glory of His kingdom He will say to His righteous sheep:

> Come, you who are blessed of My Father, inherit the kingdom prepared for you from the foundation of the world. For I was hungry, and you gave Me something to

eat; I was thirsty, and you gave Me something to drink; I was a stranger, and you invited Me in; naked, and you clothed Me; I was sick, and you visited Me; I was in prison, and you came to Me ... Truly I say to you, to the extent that you did it to one of these brothers of Mine, even the least of them, you did it to Me (Matt. 25:34-36, 40).

The church is the body of Christ. Paul wrote, "Now you are Christ's body, and individually members of it (1 Cor. 12:27). Just as Christ is the friend of sinners, also the church must be the friend of sinners. As we kneel to wash the feet of our Christian brothers and sisters, righteous and fallen, we wash the feet of the Lord. As we wash the feet of the stranger, the poor, and the prisoner, we wash the feet of the Lord.

SERVICE *AND* WORSHIP

The apostle Paul wrote to Timothy, the pastor of the church at Ephesus, regarding the qualifications for widows who wish to receive assistance from the church. He wrote:

> Do not let a widow under sixty years old be taken into the number, and not unless she has been the wife of one man, well reported for good works: if she has brought up children, if she has lodged strangers, *if she has washed the saints' feet*, if she has relieved the afflicted, if she has diligently followed every good work (1 Timothy 5:9-10).

Many New Testament scholars believe that this reference to foot-washing is to an act of hospitality common in the Ancient Near East, rather than to an act of worship in the Christian church. While it is apparent that Paul lists foot-washing among other acts of hospitality, this does not exclude the possibility that Jesus' act of foot-washing would have given the common act of foot-washing greater significance. Would not the widows of the church seek to emulate the Divine Servant? Jesus used familiar rites to establish Christian sacraments. The Lord's Supper was established from the familiar elements of the Passover. As he raised the bread and cup, Jesus said, "This is my body . . . this is my blood." Baptisms and washings were common among Jewish religious practices. But Jesus said, "He who has believed and has been baptized shall be saved" (Mark 16:16). Foot-washing, even as an act of hospitality, would have greater significance among Christians because of the example of Jesus. Foot-washing is presented as an act of hospitality in which the guest is refreshed and the one who washes the feet experiences redemptive cleansing. Foot-washing is more than a common act of hospitality; more that an act of humility; more than a metaphor for Christian service. Foot-washing is Spirit-movement towards the altar.

OBSERVANCE OF FOOT-WASHING

In many Pentecostal churches, the observance of foot-washing has traditionally been in conjunction with the celebration of the Lord's Supper. James L. Cross suggested that the Lord's Supper and foot-washing should be understood as a single sacrament in two parts. He wrote, "One is equally as binding as the other, and the serving of Communion is not enough in itself. There must of necessity also be the washing of the saints' feet" (COGE, 19 Jun 1961). The Gospel of John presents foot-washing within the theological context of water baptism *and* the Lord's Supper. Therefore, it follows that foot-washing can rightly be observed in conjunction with both water baptism and the Lord's Supper, or it can even be observed as a sacrament in its own right. A proper understanding of foot-washing must allow for multiple interpretations, none of which excludes the others. Foot-washing is a sacrament that lends itself to a wide variety of occasions and experiences.

Foot-washing may be observed as a sacrament of sanctification and reconciliation. Jesus washed the feet of His disciples because He wanted them to be "completely clean." Foot-washing could be an excellent opportunity for brothers and sisters in the Lord to confess their sins to one another, embrace each other in the love of God, and allow the Holy Spirit to cleanse the sins of the community, as well as the sins of the individual. Foot-washing may be observed to signify confession and remission of postbaptismal sins. Whereas, water baptism is an unrepeatable act of initiation, foot-washing should be repeated often as a sacrament of cleansing. Foot-washing serves as a sign of grace that the fallen may be restored. Therefore, foot-washing could be scheduled in conjunction with water baptismal services. After all baptismal candidates have been baptized "for the remission of sins," the pastor could issue a call for repentance and offer an opportunity for penitent sinners to come to the altar, confess their sins, and have their feet washed by the pastor or other congregational leaders.

Repentance and confession must become a significant part of any church that seeks a renewing encounter with the Spirit (Acts 3:19). Many times our worship is hindered because we grieve or quench the Holy Spirit (Eph. 4:30; 1 Thes. 5:19). Further, the witness of Christ is diminished when the church fails to reflect the character of our Lord. Christ has called His church to be a model of unity and peace, but too often we have failed. Our Lord has commanded that we are to love and pray for our enemies, and He has called us to be "ambassadors of reconciliation" (2 Cor. 5:20). In his Sermon on the Mount, Jesus said:

> . . . I say to you that everyone who is angry with his brother shall be guilty before the court; and whoever says to his brother, "You good-for-nothing," shall be guilty before the supreme court; and whoever says, "You fool," shall be guilty enough to go into the fiery hell. Therefore if you are presenting your offering at the altar, and there remember that your brother has something against you, leave your offering there before the altar and go; first be reconciled to your brother, and then come and present your offering (Matt. 5:22-24).

Our Lord has taught us that we can offer worship that is unacceptable. We cannot approach the altar of God with an acceptable sacrifice when our hearts are filled with anger and bitterness, or conflicts and schisms. Often, these conflicts involve entire communities and are grounded in ethnic, economic, and geopolitical issues. The church must transcend the conflicts of this world and be a prophetic people in whom the world may see the redemption of God. In this regard, foot-washing can become a significant prophetic act in which the grace of God is conveyed and demonstrated.

Some years ago, I was pastoring a church in a rural city of the American South. This city has a long history of racial tension. During a week of revival services, I scheduled a choir from a local African-American church to sing in our services. On this evening, the Spirit of the Lord was moving and everyone seemed to be enjoying the music of our guest choir. During the service, I was impressed by the Holy Spirit to wash the feet of my African-American colleague and brother. I sent for a towel and basin and asked permission to wash his feet. He agreed. As our two combined congregations watched, I bowed before my brother and washed his feet as a symbol of reconciliation between our two communities of faith. The weeks that followed were filled with much trouble for me and the church I served. When I washed the feet of my black brother, some of the members of the church became angry. The act of foot-washing became a prophetic confrontation in that congregation. Many believers were forced to acknowledge their sin of racial prejudice, but they were unprepared to repent and be sanctified. Some months later, I resigned from that pastorate. About two years later, I received a telephone call from one of the congregational leaders of that church. During the course of our conversation, he informed me that several African-American families had been received into the membership of the church. The church was becoming a prospering multicultural congregation. He said, "It would not have happened without your example of reconciliation." Foot-washing is a sacrament of grace that prophetically confronts the human heart so that our conflicts may be healed. Through the Spirit of grace, foot-washing forms a sanctified community.

Foot-washing may be observed in ceremonies in which fallen members and ministers are restored to fellowship. When a Christian falls into such sin that the discipline of the church requires that person to be excluded from membership, the whole body is injured. Likewise, when a pastor or other minister of the church falls into such sin, the integrity of the whole ministry is injured. Too often, the church fails in the ministry of restoration because of the pain associated with such events. At other times, restoration fails due to the unwillingness of the fallen minister (or member) to demonstrate humility and repentance. However, every effort should be made to effect healing and the restoration of integrity and fellowship. In many cases, such ethical failures become a public scandal. Because the failure is public, the work of restoration must likewise be public. Foot-washing could become an important element in the public restoration of the fallen. In such cases, those who are to be restored to fellowship and ministry should present themselves at the altar and before the assembled congregation. After a time of prayer, the presiding officer — a pastor, or bishop — would then perform the foot-washing as a sign of forgiveness and restoration.

Foot-washing may be observed as a sacrament of commission. Because foot-washing has been associated with the mission and ministry of the church, it would be appropriate that the foot-washing service be presented in terms of Christian mission. Christians must be reminded that our sanctuaries and auditoriums are places of rest and nourishment, but we must leave our places of worship to do the work of Christ. It is into the fields and highways that we are called. Foot-washing should be a perpetual reminder that Christ expects our feet to become dirty from our travels throughout this world. The feet of holy men and women are the instruments by which the gospel is to be carried into our neighborhoods, hospitals, schools, prisons, and everywhere that lost and hurting people can be found. The apostle Paul exclaimed, "How beautiful are the feet of those who bring good news of good things!" (Rom. 10:15). Each time we receive Christ in the Lord's Supper, we should be reminded of the Great Commission.

Foot-washing should be observed at ordination ceremonies. Jesus washed the feet of His disciples and sent them into the world.

Since foot-washing exemplifies authentic Christian ministry it should be incorporated into public worship services in which men and women are affirmed and credentialed by the church for ministry. Ministerial candidates should station themselves at the altar, and before the congregation. There the candidates are charged for ministry by their respective ordaining authority. Then these ministerial candidates should have their feet washed by their respective bishop, or ordaining council, as a commissioning act.

Foot-washing should also be incorporated into services and ceremonies in which ministers are installed into new places of ministry. When pastors arrive at a new place of ministry, a foot-washing ceremony should be performed as an act of commission and dedication. New pastors should have their feet washed by the officer of installation, or by the leaders of the local church. This act would signify that the congregation has accepted their new pastor, and pledges their love, prayers, and support. In turn, pastors should wash the feet of the members of their new congregation as an act of devotion and service to them. Foot-washing should be similarly incorporated into the installation services of regional bishops (superintendents, etc.) and denominational leaders. By doing so, ministers demonstrate that those who lead the church are in fact bond-servants of the church (Mark 10:42-45).

Foot-washing may be observed as a sacrament of Christian unity. Through many years of service as pastor, I have had the pleasure of serving in various ecumenical ministerial associations. On many occasions I have been involved in planning special community services such as the National Day of Prayer, Holy Week observances, and Christian unity events. These community services are attended by Christians from various traditions. Sadly, many churches prohibit their members from sharing in Holy Communion among nonmembers. So, it is often difficult to conduct an ecumenical worship service that includes Holy Communion. I have often suggested that ecumenical services include the observance of foot-washing. In most cases, this suggestion has been enthusiastically received. I remember one such service in which the local Catholic priest and Methodist pastor washed each other's feet. On another occasion, during a National Day of Prayer observance, about thirty pastors, representing various denominations, gathered on the steps of the county courthouse to publicly wash each other's feet. The observance of foot-washing serves as a visible expression of the church as the fellowship of the Holy Spirit in which grace is extended to all brothers and sisters in Christ.

7

RECOVERING LOST TREASURES

There are many challenges that face Pentecostal churches as we transition into the second century of the movement. Many of these challenges are not unlike the challenges of other renewal movements throughout the history of the church. Early Pentecostals inherited a rich deposit of Christian tradition. From time to time, the church loses a treasure. The parable of the lost coin teaches us that we must be very careful to guard the treasures with which we have been blessed. The woman had ten coins.

> Or what woman, if she has ten silver coins and loses one coin, does not light a lamp and sweep the house and search carefully until she finds it? When she has found it, she calls together her friends and neighbors, saying, "Rejoice with me, for I have found the coin which I had lost!" (Lu. 15:8-9).

Ironic as it may seem, renewal movements often look back for inspiration and guidance as they engage the future. This is especially true for those who seek reformation, or revival, within the Christian church. Renewal movements seek to recover something that has been lost. The Pentecostal Movement was birthed as sincere believers sought to recover the apostolic faith and the power of the Holy Spirit.

The first great treasure is the revelation of God as Holy Trinity. Human redemption is accomplished as God the Father embraces us with God's two hands — Son and Spirit. This divine embrace lifts us out of the corruption of this present age and places us in heavenly places. We must be careful to preserve this treasure of the faith. From the perspective of a Pentecostal, it seems that all too often the church has presented God the Father with one hand (Christ) reaching out to humanity, but the other hand (Spirit) is tied behind God's back. The Pentecostal "full gospel" affirms the ancient Christian faith that the Son and the Spirit are one with the Father. The Father's saving embrace is fully expressed in the Incarnation and Pentecost. Salvation is receiving Christ and the Holy Spirit.

Another treasure is the church — redeemed humanity in fellowship with the Holy Trinity. The church is the "body of Christ" and the "fellowship of the Holy Spirit." The church is our mother, from whom we receive nourishment and nurture. She is to be honored. There are many challenges presently before us as it relates to our understanding of the church. Some Christians don't even like the term. They claim there is too much negative historical baggage associated with the term. It is because of the church's baggage that the Spirit continuously works to renew the church. A full hearing of the church's history will reveal its sins, but also its glory. For Pentecostals, the church is essential in God's redemptive plan. The church is the dwelling of the Holy Spirit and is empowered by the Spirit for mission. So, instead of deconstructing the church, we should seek to renew her. Pentecostal spirituality is expressed as Christ and Spirit in the Church. The sacraments are redemptive treasures. The sacraments are visible and physical expressions of God's redemptive work in our lives. Sacraments call us to the altar so that we may present our bodies to God as a "living and holy sacrifice."

Sacraments tell the story of redemption. As we participate in sacramental worship, we are washed and cleansed, we are nourished and healed, and we confess and are forgiven. As I have demonstrated, early Pentecostals enthusiastically embraced the sacraments. The "full gospel" means that the whole counsel of God's Word is to be proclaimed and practiced.

As we seek to make church "relevant," we have witnessed the inclusion of liturgical dance, living drama, and even mime in worship services. I embrace these forms of visual worship. However, the sacraments should not be viewed as archaic, or incidental, forms of worship. Worship must be more than entertainment. Worship must be a transformative encounter with God. The sacraments are the physical means of this encounter.

In 2013 a detailed assessment of the worship beliefs and practices of Church of God congregations in the South Georgia region was conducted. The assessment involved nineteen local churches with five hundred, thirty-one respondents from ministers and laity. The goal of this project was to assess how Pentecostals view the sacraments and determine how the celebration of the sacraments enriches Pentecostal spirituality. A summary of the assessment reveals the following conclusions.

> The altar continues to be a significant sacred space in Pentecostal worship and younger believers (under 35 years old) are more active in the altars.
>
> Tongues-speech is a significant spiritual experience for less than one-half of the respondents. This is especially true among those who are under thirty-five years old. However, tongues-speech, as a "sign of God's presence" or as "the initial physical evidence" of Spirit baptism, was strongly affirmed. It seems that the respondents are committed to the significance of tongues-speech in Pentecostal worship, even if most of them have not experienced the phenomena.
>
> The sacraments are more than mere symbols. Pentecostal worshipers have an intuitive understanding that God is present in sacramental worship. Sacraments are believed to be sanctifying gifts and sources of grace.
>
> The anointed touch – prayer for the sick by anointing with oil and/or the laying on hands – is the most common sacramental observance among these congregations. The anointed touch is a weekly occurrence and most Pentecostals strongly agree that it is a biblical method for healing the sick.
>
> Water baptism is believed to be necessary and signifies new birth in Christ. However, most pastors are not

baptizing new converts and many churches have not had a water baptism in many years.

The Lord's Supper is strongly affirmed as a sacramental rite in which Christ and Spirit are present. Many Pentecostals have been taught that the Lord's Supper is memorial observance, not a means of grace. Pentecostal worshipers have an intuitive awareness of the presence of Christ and Spirit in the Lord's Supper in spite of being taught otherwise. In fact, a surprising result indicates that Pentecostals encounter the presence of God in the Lord's Supper to the same degree they encounter God's presence in tongues-speech. Celebration of the Lord's Supper is relegated to a quarterly or bi-annual event. Pentecostal worshipers desire to celebrate the Lord's Supper more often. Pastors tend to agree that the meal should be celebrated at the altar. In an interview, one pastor commented that observing the Supper in the pews seemed to be done without much reflection by the communicants; but at the altar the communicants seemed to "savor the moment."

Foot-washing is rarely practiced, and pastors are not teaching about this sacred act. The effect is that foot-washing is not understood as an essential act of Pentecostal worship. Further, interviews with the pastors revealed that they had never been taught that foot-washing was a sign of cleansing.

Pastors have a vital role in teaching and proper administration of the sacraments. Pentecostal worshipers will positively respond when pastors engage in informed theological preaching and teaching. Further, the results indicate that pastors are more confident in leading the administration of the sacraments when they have a firm theological basis to celebrate these rites. Also, pastors must be more intentional in scheduling and planning sacramental rites. The results reveal a disconnection between thought and practice. Even as the sacraments are affirmed as significant encounters, sacramental observances are not regularly scheduled.

Sacraments should not be viewed as archaic, or incidental, forms of worship. Worship must be more than entertainment. Worship must be a transformative encounter with God. The sacraments are the physical means of this encounter.

The woman had ten coins, but lost one. She was not satisfied with the nine remaining coins. She sought to recover the lost coin. If we are to be faithful to our Pentecostal heritage, we must never allow any treasure of the "full gospel" to be lost. Just as our Pentecostal patriarchs and matriarchs sought to recover an encounter with the Holy Spirit, we must be diligent to search the house for any lost treasure. Pentecostal pastors must hold fast to their role as the primary teachers and worship leaders of the church. We must be students of the Scriptures, searching the Scriptures for every redemptive treasure. This is an ongoing task that is essential to the renewal of the church. The sacraments have become the lost treasure of many Pentecostal churches. We have treasures remaining. However, we must not be satisfied until we recover all lost treasures. Then we can rejoice.

BIBLIOGRAPHY

Assemblies of God Publications: Pre WW II DVD. Springfield, MO: Flower Pentecostal Heritage Center, 2006.

Book of Doctrines. Cleveland, TN: Church of God Publishing House, 1922.

Book of General Instructions for the Ministry and Membership. Cleveland, TN: Church of God Publishing House, 1927.

Book of Minutes: A compiled history of the work of the General Assemblies of the Church of God. Cleveland, TN: Church of God Publishing House, 1922.

Catechism of the Catholic Church, 2nd edition. Washington, DC: United States Catholic Conference, 1994, 1997.

Church of God Publications 1901-1923 DVD. Cleveland, TN: Dixon Pentecostal Research Center, 2008.

Conkin, Paul K. *Cane Ridge: America's Pentecost.* Madison, WI: The University of Wisconsin Press, 1990.

Seymour, William J. *The Azusa Papers.* Jawbone Digital. Kindle Edition. 2011.

Skarsaune, Oskar. *In the Shadow of the Temple: Jewish Influences on Early Christianity.* Downers Grove, IL: InterVarsity Press, 2002.

Staniloae, Dumitru. *The Sanctifying Mysteries.* Brookline, MA: Holy Cross Orthodox Press, 2012.

Tipei, John Fleter. *The Laying on of Hands in the New Testament.* Lanham, MD: University Press of America, Inc., 2009.

The Pentecostal Holiness Advocate 1917-1924 CD. Oklahoma City: International Pentecostal Holiness Church, 2005.

Tomberlin, Daniel. *Pentecostal Sacraments: Encountering God at the Altar. Revised Edition.* 2015.

Tomlinson, A. J. *The Last Great Conflict.* Cleveland, TN: Press of Walter E. Rodgers, 1913.

Wesley, John. *The Works of John Wesley, 3rd edition.* Albany, OR: Ages Software, 1997.

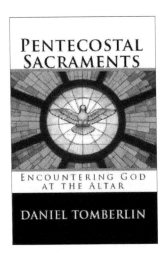

PENTECOSTAL SACRAMENTS

ENCOUNTERING GOD
AT THE ALTAR

DANIEL TOMBERLIN

Daniel Tomberlin dares to say that Baptism, the Lord's Supper, Footwashing and Anointing with oil are all sacramental means of grace enabling us to remember, experience and anticipate the mysteries of salvation. Together they symbolize the Christian's journey from initiation to glorification and our need for continual cleansing along the way. Drawing from ecumenical dialogues, scholarly research, devotional reflections and 30 years of pastoral experience, Tomberlin adds valuable insights to the discussion on what it means to be Pentecostal and how Spirit filled believers view the practices Christ instituted.

It is a pleasure to commend this book for personal reflection, believing it will prove valuable in stimulating further discussion on the place and practice of sacraments in Pentecostal worship.

Dr. Mark Williams, General Overseer
Church of God – Cleveland, Tennessee

DanielTomberlin.net
dan@danieltomberlin.net

Made in the USA
Lexington, KY
10 February 2018